lonely planet

POCKET BILBAO & SAN SEBASTIÁN

Isabel Albiston

Contents

Top: Donostia-San Sebastián Gros (p133)
Bottom: Plaza Nueva, Bilbao (p41)

Explore Bilbao 33

Explore San Sebastián 97

Pintxos (Basque tapas)

ROM TOP LEFT: ASIFE/SHUTTERSTOCK ©, RICARDO ALGAR/ SHUTTERSTOCK ©, IVAN VIEITO GARCIA/SHUTTERSTOCK ©

Toolkit 157

★ Top Experiences

Worth a Trip

The Journey Begins Here

With its cutting-edge architecture and thriving cultural scene, Bilbao is an exciting urban centre that feels connected to the world. But wherever you are in the city, you can see the often-mist-covered mountains that rise from either side of the river; nature is just steps away. Donostia-San Sebastián is more beautiful still, with mesmerising coastal views, leading arts festivals and restaurants that rank among the world's best. Between them lies a stretch of coast where protected woodlands and wetlands meet flysch rock formations, formed 100 million years ago.

Isabel Albiston

@isabel_albiston

Isabel is a travel writer who spends as much time as she can in the Basque Country.

Monte Urgull, Donostia-San Sebastián (p108)

THOMAS DUTOUR/SHUTTERSTOCK ©

THE BEST

Art Experiences

Bilbao's star attraction is its world-famous art museum, but beyond the Guggenheim, the Basque Country is packed with opportunities to experience art and see works by emerging and established artists.

View works by some of the world's leading artists at the **Museo Guggenheim Bilbao**, the region's standout art museum. (p52)

Take a short boat trip to **Isla de Santa Clara** to see a sculpted seabed art installation in a hollowed-out lighthouse. (p108; pictured above left)

Stroll among Eduardo Chillida's sculptures, which emerge from the grass-like trees in the garden setting of **Chillida Leku**. (p142)

See pieces by Basque sculptor **Jorge Oteiza** at the Parte Vieja waterfront and Iglesia de San Vicente. (p111)

Check out the work of emerging contemporary artists at the **galleries** in San Sebastián's Gros neighbourhood. (p138)

Discover the collections of classical, contemporary and Basque art at Bilbao's **Museo de Bellas Artes**. (p61; pictured above right)

Right: Sculpture by Jorge Oteiza, Parte Vieja (p11

THE BEST

Museum Experiences

From football and fashion to the sea, the interactive exhibits at a series of excellent museums provide an entertaining experience of the themes they cover. Sensitive subjects are treated with care.

Understand the history of the devastating bombing of Gernika and view thought-provoking displays on the themes of reconciliation and peace at the **Museo de la Paz**. (p82)

Learn all about the history and successes of Bilbao's football team **Athletic Club** with an entertaining museum visit and a behind-the-scenes stadium tour. (p55)

Admire dramatically lit pieces by fashion designer Cristóbal Balenciaga, who was born in Getaria, at the town's suitably fabulous **museum**. (p87; pictured above right)

Learn all about Bilbao's marine history at **Itsasmuseum**, at the site of the former shipbuilding works. (p61; pictured above left)

Explore the exhibits on history of the Basque people's relationship to the sea at the **Aquarium**. (p104)

Right: Athletic Club (p55)

FROM LEFT: SAIKO3P/SHUTTERSTOCK ©, MARK GREEN/SHUTTERSTOCK ©, YURI TURKOV/SHUTTERSTOCK ©

TITULUAK ETA GARAIKURRAK • LOS TÍTULOS

THE BEST

Outdoor Experiences

With easy access to rivers, hills and the sea, an outdoor adventure is never far away in Bilbao and Donostia-San Sebastián. Pick up your surfboard or put on your hiking boots and head outside.

Take a **kayaking trip** down the River Nervión, and view the Guggenheim from the water. (p60)

Glide off the cliffs of Getxo on a tandem **paragliding flight** (p77; pictured above left), with views over the Cantabrian Sea.

Feel the burn as you cycle up **Monte Jaizkibel**, one of the Basque Country's legendary uphill cycles. The scenery is worth it. (p152; pictured above right)

Hike along the coast from Donostia-San Sebastián to **Pasaia**, gazing at the craggy coastline and the sea beyond. (p152)

Sign up for surfing lessons in **Mundaka** or take a stand-up paddleboarding trip across the estuary. (p92)

Cross the bridge and climb the steps to reach the island hermitage of **San Juan de Gaztelugatxe**. (p88)

Right: Monte Ulia, Donostia-San Sebastián (p139)

THE BEST

Architectural Experiences

Bilbao's newer buildings are designed in an architectural style that references the city's industrial past, and they have to be seen to be understood. If elegant belle époque design is more your style, you'll love Donostia-San Sebastián.

Dare to look down as you stroll across the *pasarela* walkway of the **Puente Colgante**, the world's first transporter bridge, which links Getxo and Portugalete. (p72)

Admire the columns and a balustraded terrace of the **Galerías de Punta Begoña**, a landmark building that formed part of Getxo's defensive wall. (p78)

Take a tour to learn about the architecture of **Euskalduna Palace** or get tickets to a concert. The building is designed to look like a ship under construction. (p62; pictured above right)

Explore the columns and spaces of **Azkuna Zentroa** (also known as Alhóndiga), a former wine store turned cultural centre. (p60; pictured above left)

Attend a performance at the archi-tectual landmark, **Kursaal**, an events venue and conference centre. (p139)

Right: Puente Colgante (p72)

THE BEST

Food & Drink Experiences

Whether snacking on *pintxos* (Basque tapas), feasting on seafood or splashing out on a Michelin-starred meal, experiencing the outstanding food and drink of the Basque coast is one of the great pleasures of visiting the region.

Order freshly caught fish at the outdoor terrace of one of the waterside restaurants in **Pasai San Pedro**. (p152)

Learn to make traditional Basque dishes and prepare *pintxos* at a cooking class with **Mimo Bite The Experience**. (p126)

Feast on seafood in the former fishing village of **Puerto Viejo** in Getxo and then drink *txakoli* wine outside the local taverns. (p78; pictured above left)

Graze your way around Donostia-San Sebastián's **Parte Vieja** on a *pintxo* bar crawl, tasting a different morsel in each place. (p110)

Shop for fresh produce and then head to the *pintxo* bars for snacks at Bilbao's **Mercado de la Ribera**. (p40; pictured above right)

Eat at one of Hondarribia's outstanding restaurants and then hit the bars of **Calle San Pedro**. (p153)

Right: Colourful buildings, Hondarribia (p145)

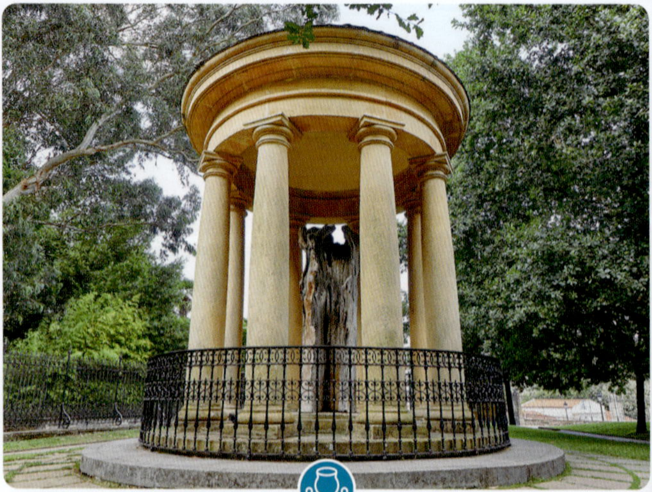

Árbol de Gernika (p83)

THE BEST

Basque Culture Experiences

Basque culture is steeped in mythology, folklore and intriguing traditions, which continue to be present in everyday life. Get to know the Basque people by experiencing their music, sport and history.

See the hallowed **Árbol de Gernika**, the symbolic oak tree under which Basques have had political discussions since medieval times. Afterwards, look inside the Assembly House outside where the tree stands. (p83)

Learn everything about Basque history and culture through the exhibits and artefacts of the **San Telmo Museoa**, partly housed in a former convent. (p101)

Find out about the Basque whaling ships of bygone days and see a replica of such a vessel being reconstructed using original building techniques at the **Albaola Foundation**. (p148)

Discover how Basques lived from the Paleolithic period through to the Middle Ages at Bilbao's **Arkeologi Museoa**. Use virtual reality goggles to view the Neolithic artwork of nearby caves. (p37)

Best for Kids

Brace yourself as sharks swim overhead and an array of fish approach from all sides in the transparent tunnel of the **Aquarium** (p104).

Learn about 100-million-year-old flysch rock formations and how they might be proof that a meteorite ended the dinosaurs as you zoom along the coast on a **boat trip** (p92).

Ride the funicular railway up **Monte Igueldo** (p122), and then get your adrenaline pumping on rollercoasters at the hilltop funfair.

Make sandcastles and swim in the sea at **Playa de la Concha** (p120), and then go for an ice cream.

Paddle a **kayak** (p60) down the Ría del Nervión, floating under bridges and taking in views of Bilbao's most famous sights along the way.

Best for Free

Hike over the cliffs from Donostia-San Sebastián to **Pasaia** (p152), with breathtaking views along the way.

Stroll the beachside promenade, cool off with a dip in the sea, relax on the sand, or join in a beach volleyball or football game at **Playa de la Concha** (p120).

View exhibitions, relax in the meditation area or head to the roof terrace to admire the views at the **Tabakalera** (p135) cultural centre.

Walk along the waterfront via Playa de la Concha and Playa de Ondarreta to see Eduardo Chillida's sculptures, **Peine del Viento** (Wind Comb; p126).

Climb to the top of **Monte Serantes** (p79) for dizzying views over Bilbao and the mountains beyond.

Three Perfect Days

Wear comfortable walking shoes to explore Bilbao and Donostia-San Sebastián. Strolling between sights is a joy in these walkable cities. Be sure to stop for *pintxos* (Basque tapas) along the way.

Plaza Nueva, Bilbao (p41)

DAY ONE

Only Have One Day?

MORNING

Start your day in Bilbao with a stroll along the river, crossing **Zubizuri** (p59; pictured) and continuing to the **Museo Guggenheim Bilbao** (p52), the city's unmissable art museum.

AFTERNOON

Walk through **Parque de Doña Casilda de Iturrizar** (p63) to the **Museo de Bellas Artes** (p61). Next, pop into the **Azkuna Zentroa** (p60) and browse for souvenirs in **DendAZ** (p67).

EVENING

Head to the **Casco Viejo**, where you can spend the evening snacking your way from one *pintxo* bar to the next. Be sure to hit up the bars of **Plaza Nueva** (p41), including **Gure Toki** (p44).

DAY TWO

A Weekend Trip

MORNING

Kick off a day in Donostia-San Sebastián with a crash course in Basque culture at **San Telmo Museoa** (p101). Or, stand surrounded by fish at the city's **Aquarium** (p104). Finish the morning with a hike up **Monte Urgull** (p108).

AFTERNOON

Sample *pintxos* in the Parte Vieja and then head to **Playa de la Concha** (p120) for people-watching and swimming. Next, walk along the promenade to see the **Peine del Viento** (p126; pictured) sculptures, stopping to take in the views from **Jardines de Miramar** (p128).

EVENING

Cross the river to Gros. Have a *pintxo* in **Bergara Bar** (p140) before hitting the bars of Calle Zabaleta.

DAY THREE

A Short Break

MORNING

Skip the motorway from Bilbao to Donostia-San Sebastián and instead take a slow, spectacular drive along the Basque coast. Visit Portugalete's **Puente Colgante** (p72) and then head east to **San Juan de Gaztelugatxe** (p88). If time allows, hike to the **Matxitxako lighthouses** (p89).

AFTERNOON

Make your way to Lekeitio for lunch at **Mesón Arropain** (p94) and then take a siesta on the beach. If the tide is low, walk out to the **Isla de San Nicolás** (p93; pictured).

EVENING

Continue east to Getaria to see the fashion at the **Cristóbal Balenciaga Museoa** (p87). Finish up with seafood at Getaria's port.

If You Have More Time

Check what's on in Bilbao and Donostia-San Sebastián during your stay, particularly at the **Kursaal** (p139), **Euskalduna Palace** (p62) and **Teatro Arriaga** (p40).

In Bilbao, see the city from different perspectives with a funicular railway ride up **Artxanda** (p60) and a **kayaking trip** (p60) down the river. In nearby Getxo, you can **hike along the coast** (p76) or take a tandem **paragliding flight** (p77) from the cliffs.

On the slow road from Bilbao to Donostia-San Sebastián, stop for a surfing lesson in **Mundaka** (p92) and take an inland detour to visit the museums in **Gernika** (p82). Spot migratory birds from the hides and viewing platforms of the **Urdaibai Bird Center** (p92), and then see the cliffs of the flysch coast on a hike or **boat trip** (p92).

In Donostia-San Sebastián, go **surfing** (p127), take a **cooking lesson** (p126) or walk along the coast to **Pasaia** (p152).

Surfers, Donostia-San Sebastián (p92)

A City Day Trip

Take the bus or drive from Donostia-San Sebastián to Hondarribia near the French border. Start at the *casco histórico*, inhaling the scent of jasmine as you stroll the cobbled streets. Walk, drive or cycle up to the **Santuario de Guadalupe** (p153) for spectacular views.

Have lunch at one of the city's outstanding restaurants and then head to **Playa de Hondarribia** (p152) to relax on the sand or swim, or take a quick ferry ride to the beach at **Hendaye** (p153; pictured in background) in France. Back in Hondarribia, finish with a drink on lively **Calle San Pedro** (p153).

On a Rainy Day

On a rainy day in Bilbao, you can visit the city's museums. As well as the **Museo Guggenheim Bilbao** (p52) and the **Museo de Bellas Artes** (p61), you can visit Athletic Club's home ground and **museum** (p55) and learn about Bilbao's maritime history at **Itsasmuseum** (p61; pictured). Next, take the metro to the **Arkeologi Museoa** (p37) in Casco Viejo for a deep dive into local history.

In Donostia-San Sebastián, there's the **San Telmo Museoa** (p101) and the **Aquarium** (p104) to visit. You can also check out **Tabakalera** (p135), with exhibition spaces and a cinema.

Get Prepared

BOOK AHEAD

Three months before
Book your accommodation. Reserve even earlier if visiting during July and August.

One month before
Book a table at top dining rooms like **Mina Restaurante** (p45) in Bilbao and **Amelia** (p129) in Donostia-San Sebastián.

One week before
Book online tickets for the **Museo Guggenheim Bilbao** (p52) to avoid queues. Make other bookings like tours and concert tickets.

Manners Matter

Be sensitive to the Basque people's sense of identity. Avoid referring to the Basque Country or its people as Spanish.

Making an effort to say a few words in Basque is appreciated. Greet people with *kaixo* ('hello' in Basque) and when you leave, say *agur* (goodbye).

Skip discussions about Basque politics unless you really know what you're talking about.

Euskal Herria

Many Basques see their identity as strongly tied to the region they call Euskadi (País Vasco in Spanish or the Basque Country in English). Euskadi, or the Basque Autonomous Community, officially includes the provinces of Biscay (and its capital Bilbao), Gipuzkoa (and its capital Donostia-San Sebastián) and Álava (and its capital Vitoria-Gasteiz). However, many Basques consider Euskal Herria ('the land of Basque speakers') to more broadly include Navarra and three provinces in southern France.

Things to Know

Language The Basque Country has two official languages, Spanish and Basque (Euskera). Information is usually provided in both. Most Basques speak both languages; all speak Spanish.

City Names San Sebastián is known as Donostia in Basque. Most locals prefer to call the city by its Basque name, and that's the name used by bus companies, too – good to keep in mind if you are catching the bus there from the airport. The Basque name for Bilbao is Bilbo, but Bilbao is more commonly used.

Cash Apps The app Bizum is widely used to make payments in the Basque Country. However, to use it, you must have an account with a Spanish IBAN (ie an account with a Spanish bank).

TIPPING

Tipping is almost always optional but is usual in restaurants. Staff might expect a larger tip in more touristy places, but use your discretion.

- **5-10%** Restaurants
- **Unusual** Bars
- **Unusual** Hotel staff
- **Optional** Taxis but most locals round up

DAILY BUDGET

BUDGET: Less than €200

- Dorm bed in a Bilbao hostel: **€30–50**
- Meal made with fresh market produce: **€5–10**
- Museum admission: **€3–10**
- Glass of *txakoli* wine at a Casco Viejo bar: **€2–3**

MIDRANGE: €200–400

- Double room in a Donostia-San Sebastián *pensión* (guesthouse): **€120–250**
- *Pintxos* (Basque tapas) in the Parte Vieja: **€3–5**
- Entrance to the Aquarium: **€14**
- Coffee and cake at a cafe: **€5–8**

TOP END: More than €400

- A night at a high-end hotel: from **€200**
- Tasting menu at a fine-dining restaurant with wine: **€150**
- Admission to the Museo Guggenheim Bilbao: **€18**
- *Pintxo* cooking class with lunch: **€195**

Currency
Euro (€)

Languages
Basque (Euskera), Spanish (Castilian)

Time
Central European Time (GMT/UTC plus one hour)

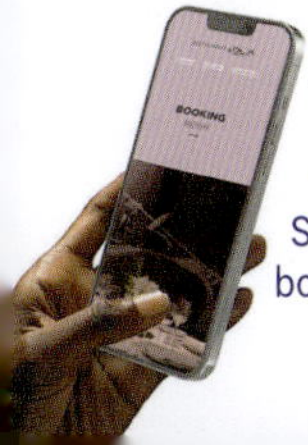

NISSRINE MAHMOUD/SHUTTERSTOCK ©

TIP

If you'd like to book a meal in one of the world-renowned, three-Michelin-starred restaurants near Bilbao and Donostia-San Sebastián, plan months in advance. Each has its own online booking system, with advanced reservations opening at different times.

When To Go

With a wealth of indoor and outdoor attractions and a packed events calendar year-round, any time is a good time to visit Bilbao and Donostia-San Sebastián.

Summer is the most popular time to visit, for sunny days on the beach and the Aste Nagusia fiestas. Early autumn is a wonderful time of year. The sea is warm enough for swimming, but the beaches are less crowded. Later, the turning leaves transform the city trees with colour.

Winter is darker and wetter, but street parties and festivals continue nonetheless. For serious surfers, winter brings the biggest waves. The weather stays chilly until March, but by early spring, the cliffs are carpeted with wildflowers once again.

The Big Events

January On the **Día de San Sebastián** (20 January), the city celebrates its patron saint. The biggest event is the Tamborrada, when thousands of drummers wearing 19th-century military dress or chefs' whites parade through the city. The party kicks off with the raising of the city flag in Plaza de la Constitución.

February or March Both Bilbao and San Sebastián celebrate **Carnaval** over six days, from the Thursday before Ash Wednesday to Shrove Tuesday, with floats, parades, costumes and dancing. In Bilbao, the action centres around Casco Viejo.

August The streets of Bilbao are packed with revellers during the nine-day festival of **Aste Nagusia** (Semana Grande), which involves concerts, traditional Basque sports, parades and fireworks. The event begins with the appearance of

Bilbao & Donostia-San Sebastián Weather

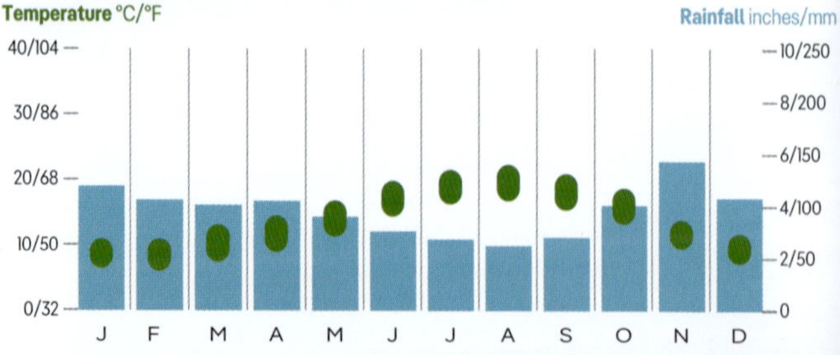

Bilbao BBK Live

Marijaia (a puppet) on the balcony of the Teatro Arriaga, and it ends with her dramatic burning. Donostia-San Sebastián celebrates its own Aste Nagusia in August too.

December For one day in December, the streets of Bilbao and Donostia-San Sebastián transform into a country fair for the **Feria de Santo Tomás**, with folk music and produce for sale. In Bilbao, stalls fill Arenal park.

Music & Culture

June Around the longest day of the year, the streets of Bilbao host the **Noche Blanca** outdoor art exhibition, with installations outside the Guggenheim.

July Bilbao's biggest musical event is **Bilbao BBK Live**, drawing top artists from around the globe.

September Donostia-San Sebastián hosts its world-renowned **International Film Festival**. Gala screenings take place in the Kursaal.

The **Festival Internacional de Folk** takes place in Getxo.

ACCOMMODATION LOWDOWN

Accommodation is more expensive in summer in Bilbao, Donostia-San Sebastián and along the coast. Many guesthouses in San Sebastián have minimum stays of two or three nights in peak season. The best months for bargains are February and March (except around Easter).

Getting There

Most visitors arrive at Bilbao airport. You can also fly into Biarritz or the small airport near Donostia-San Sebastián, or arrive from elsewhere in Europe by bus or train.

From Bilbao Airport to the City Centre

By Bus

Bus A3247 makes the 20-minute journey from the airport to Bilbao Intermodal bus station, stopping near Plaza Moyúa. It departs every 15 to 30 minutes from 6am to midnight. The stand is on the right of the terminal as you leave arrivals.

You can pay onboard (€3) or buy a ticket at the kiosk inside the terminal building, which also sells Barik cards (p28). The fare is lower if you pay with a Barik card.

Pesa (pesa.net/pesa/en/compra) buses run every 30 minutes from the airport to Donostia-San Sebastián (1¼ hours; €12.90).

By Taxi

Taxis from the airport to Bilbao's Old Town (Casco Viejo) cost around €25 to €35 depending on traffic.

By Car

Several car-hire companies offer rentals at Bilbao airport, including Sixt, Europcar, Enterprise and Hertz. Book in advance; you get better rates and have more vehicle options available.

Other Points of Entry

Bilbao Ferry Port

Brittany Ferries from Portsmouth in England and Rosslare in Ireland arrive at Bilbao ferry port in Zierbena, 21km from Bilbao city centre. For foot passengers, the nearest metro station is Santurtzi, 3km away.

Bilbao Intermodal Bus Station

Intercity buses arrive at the bus station in San Mamés. It's a 10-minute metro ride to Casco Viejo.

Getting Around

Bilbao is an easy city to get around, with many sights accessible on foot. It also has an efficient network of trams, buses and the metro for reaching scenic spots outside the centre. Donostia-San Sebastián is also a pleasure to explore on foot. For longer distances, use local buses and trains.

Bilbao Metro

Bilbao's metro (metrobilbao.eus; pictured right) is efficient and easy to use. Key stops include Casco Viejo, Plaza Moyúa and San Mamés (for the football stadium and bus station).

The metro runs towards the coast on both sides of the river, making it easy to get to the beach. Trains for both branches depart from the same platform, so check the destination on the announcement board and the front of the train.

Bilbao Trams

Operated by **Euskotren** (euskotren.eus), Bilbao's tram line runs between Basurtu in the southwest of the city and Atxuri train station. Stops include the Intermodal bus station, Museo Guggenheim Bilbao and Teatro Arriaga by the Casco Viejo.

FROM LEFT: NADIR KEKLIK/SHUTTERSTOCK ©, MARTYN JANDULA/SHUTTERSTOCK ©

ESSENTIAL APPS

For real-time updates on **Bilbobus** services, download the official app (bilbao.eus/cs/Satellite/bilbobus/es/lineas-bilbobus/bilbobus-en-tu-movil). Download the **Dbus** app for bus timetables and routes in Donostia-San Sebastián (dbus.eus/en/travelling-by-dbus/dbus-apps).

Tickets cost €1.50 (€0.73 with a Barik card) and need to be validated in the machine next to the ticket dispenser before boarding.

Bilbao Buses

Bilbobus (bilbao.eus) runs citywide bus services and can often bring you closer to your destination than the nearest metro or tram stop. However, if you are able to walk, it is possible to reach most places by metro or tram, or on foot.

Donostia-San Sebastián Buses

Dbus (dbus.eus) is the city's public bus network. The standard fare is €1.85 (€2.50 at night), payable to the bus driver. A useful route is bus 16, which connects the city centre with Monte Igueldo.

Walking

Walking is often the most efficient and enjoyable way to get around Bilbao and Donostia-San Sebastián. Lifts and mechanical moving walkways transport you to Bilbao's hilly neighbourhoods.

Cycling

Bilbao has a network of bike lanes that make cycling an option for longer trips, especially to and around the neighbourhoods of Getxo and Portugalete. You can hire a bike from **Tourné** (p62) in the city centre.

Donostia-San Sebastián has 77km of bike lanes. Hire wheels from **Sanse Bikes** or **Darwin Rentals**.

Trains & Intercity Buses

Euskotren trains run between Bilbao and Bermeo (via Mundaka), and Bilbao and Donostia-Sebastian (via Gernika, Deba and Zumaia).

The fastest public transport option from Bilbao to Donostia-San Sebastián is the bus from Bilbao's Intermodal bus station to **Donostia Bus Station** (1 hour, 15 minutes). Both **Lurralde** (lurraldebus.eus) and **Alsa** (alsa.es) run services once every one to two hours during the day.

Public Transport Essentials

Barik Card

You can save time and money by purchasing a Barik card for €3 at metro vending machines, topping it up with credit (from €5) and using it on Bilbao's metro, tram and bus lines. Barik cards are also sold at the ticket kiosk near the bus stand at Bilbao airport.

One card can be used for multiple people, and the card pays for itself after five uses. Barik cards are valid on buses and local trains elsewhere in Bizkaia (Biscay province).

When using buses, touch the Barik reader when you get on and again when you get off. On the tram, touch the card to the reader at the station before boarding only (you don't need to touch out).

You can also use a Barik card to pay for the **Puente Colgante** (p72) transporter bridge and the **Funicular de Artxanda** (p60).

Mugi Card

In Donostia-San Sebastián, the equivalent of the Barik card is the **Mugi card** (mugi.eus). However, because the card costs €5 and the reduction in the day fare is small (tickets cost €1.26 with a Mugi and €1.85 without), it is only worth buying if you plan on being in town for a while and using the bus a lot.

Night fares are the same price with or without a Mugi card (€2.50). You can buy and recharge Mugi cards at kiosks and newsagents in Donostia-San Sebastián.

It is also possible to buy bus tickets using the Dbus app.

TIP

Remember to tap the reader with your Barik card when getting off the bus in Bilbao.

TICKETS

Adult single-journey ticket prices for the Bilbao metro:

	Zone 1	Zone 2	Zone 3
Regular fare	€1.70	€1.90	€1.95
Barik card fare	€0.48	€0.57	€0.62

TRAVEL COSTS

Donostia-San Sebastián day bus fare
€1.85

Bilbao tram fare (without Barik card)
€1.50

Bilbao adult metro fare (without Barik card)
€1.70

TICKET ZONES

1

Zone 1 Bilbao city centre, from San Ignacio to Bolueta and Otxarkoaga.

2

Zone 2 To the end of the line, except on the Plentzia branch, where Zone 2 ends at Larrabasterra.

3

Zone 3 Larrabasterra to Plentzia.

A Few Surprises

Symbols of protection date from centuries past, while Bilbao's buildings show how architecture can transform an industrial city into something new.

Bilbao Metro

Bilbao's architectural riches run deep. Walk across town and you'll come across several futuristic glass-and-steel constructions emerging from the ground. Nicknamed *fosteritos* after Sir Norman Foster, the British architect who designed them, these entrances to the Bilbao's metro stations are masterpieces of modern functional design.

Eguzkilore

For Basques, the yellow *eguzkilore* flower – a type of thistle endemic to the Basque mountains – represents the sun and is a symbol of protection from evil spirits. Look out for them on the front doors of houses or worn as jewellery.

Seafaring Symbols

All along the Basque coast, churches and shrines have symbols related to the sea. These icons date from the days when sailors would pray to be kept safe before setting off into treacherous waters. Look for model boats suspended from church ceilings and holy-water fonts made from giant shells brought back from faraway seas.

Transformative Architecture

In Bilbao, symbols and reminders of the city's industrial past can be seen in much of the city's architecture, which has in turn helped transform Bilbao into the thriving cultural hub it is today. In **Parque Etxebarria** (p41), a chimney that was once part of a steel foundry stands in lush parkland, while Frank Gehry's titanium-clad design for the **Guggenheim** (p52) and the architecture of the nearby **Euskalduna Palace** (p62) both reference the former shipyards located at the site.

OFFBEAT BILBAO & DONOSTIA-SAN SEBASTIÁN

Kayak to an **offshore island** (p108) to watch waves wash over an art installation in a hollowed-out lighthouse.

Visit the reconstruction of a 16th-century **whaling ship** (p148) being built using the original tools and techniques.

See performance art at **Pabellón Número 6** (p63) and **La Terminal**, on Zorrotzaurre island.

Take a ride in a belle époque **funicular railway** (p122) to a hilltop funfair.

Eguzkilore

Parque Etxebarria, Bilbao (p41)

Explore Bilbao

Worth a Trip

Bilbao's Walking Tours

Lekeitio (p93)
JON CHICA/SHUTTERSTOCK ©

See p44
for eating, drinking and shopping listings

Explore Bilbao Old Town

Built around the original seven streets that formed Bilbao's medieval old quarter, compact Casco Viejo (Old Town) is now full of *pintxo* (Basque tapas) bars and independent shops. Come nightfall, the atmosphere on Calle Ronda (Erronda Kalea) takes on a local feel. Across the river from Casco Viejo is the area known as Bilbao la Vieja, comprising the streets near Puente la Merced, Calle San Francisco (the neighbourhood is also known as San Francisco) and Puente San Antón. Bilbao la Vieja is a culturally diverse area, with an emerging arts scene and some of Bilbao's most exciting new restaurants and bars.

Getting Around

Walk

The best way to navigate Casco Viejo's mostly pedestrianised streets is on foot. The Puente de la Ribera footbridge links Casco Viejo and Bilbao la Vieja.

Metro

The main entrance to the Casco Viejo (Zazpikaleak) metro station is at Plazuela de San Nicolás. Find a second entrance at Plaza Miguel Unamuno.

Tram

The tram follows the river, stopping at Arriaga (near Teatro Arriaga) and Ribera (opposite the Mercado de la Ribera) on the edge of Casco Viejo.

★

THE BEST

MUSEUM Arkeologi Museoa (p37)

PINTXO BAR Gure Toki (p44)

CITY VIEWS Parque Etxebarria (p41)

PRODUCE MARKET Mercado de la Ribera (p40)

STREET ART Muelle de la Merced (p43)

Casco Viejo (Old Town)
LEONARDO2011/SHUTTERSTOCK ©

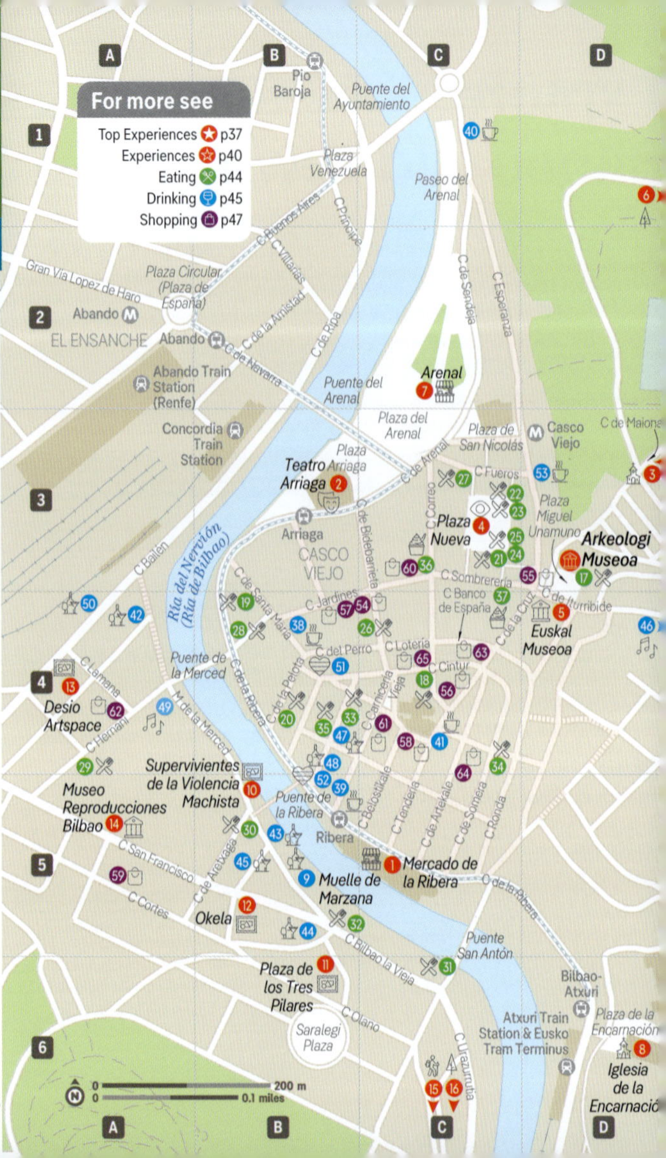
For more see
Top Experiences p37
Experiences p40
Eating p44
Drinking p45
Shopping p47
Pio Baroja
Puente del Ayuntamiento
Plaza Venezuela
Paseo del Arenal
C Buenos Aires
C Príncipe
C Villarías
Gran Vía Lopez de Haro
Plaza Circular (Plaza de España)
Abando
EL ENSANCHE
Abando
C de la Amistad
C de Navarra
C de Ripa
C de Sendeja
C Esperanza
Abando Train Station (Renfe)
Concordia Train Station
Puente del Arenal
Arenal
Plaza del Arenal
Plaza de San Nicolás
Casco Viejo
C de Maione
C de Arenal
Plaza Arriaga
Teatro Arriaga
C Fueros
Plaza Miguel Unamuno
C Correo
Plaza Nueva
Arkeologi Museoa
Arriaga
C de Bidebarrieta
CASCO VIEJO
Ría del Nervión (Ría de Bilbao)
C Bailén
C Sombrerería
C Banco de España
C de la Cruz
C de Iturribide
Euskal Museoa
C de Santa María
C Jardines
C del Perro
C Lotería
C Cintur
Puente de la Merced
C de la Ribera
C de la Pelota
C Carnicería Vieja
C Lamana
C Hernani
M. de la Merced
Desio Artspace
Supervivientes de la Violencia Machista
Museo Reproducciones Bilbao
Puente de la Ribera
Ribera
C Belostikale
C Tendería
C de Artekale
C de Somera
C Ronda
C San Francisco
C de Aretxaga
Mercado de la Ribera
C de la Ribera
Muelle de Marzana
C Cortes
Okela
C Bilbao la Vieja
Puente San Antón
Plaza de los Tres Pilares
C Olano
Saralegi Plaza
C Urazurrutia
Bilbao-Atxuri
Atxuri Train Station & Eusko Tram Terminus
Plaza de la Encarnación
Iglesia de la Encarnació
0 200 m
0 0.1 miles
A B C D
1 2 3 4 5 6

★ TOP EXPERIENCE

Arkeologi Museoa

Bilbao's Archaeology Museum takes in some 100,000 years of the region's history. Displays of objects excavated from nearby caves and other sites, alongside models showing the evolution of the dwellings and villages in which local people lived, take visitors on a journey through time.

MAP P36 **D3**

Prehistory

To view the exhibits in chronological order, start on the 2nd floor. Here, the journey begins with panels showing details of Palaeolithic art found on the walls of nearby caves, including images of deer, bison, horses and bears. Put on the VR goggles to take a virtual tour through the chambers of Armintxe cave in Lekeitio.

Next, check out the displays of objects found in the caves of Santamamiñe and Lumentxa, including arrowheads and deer teeth once worn as a necklace. Don't miss the stone engraved with a figure of a horse, dating from between 15,000 and 9000 BCE.

Exhibits from the Bronze Age include a model of a fortified hill fort.

The Roman Period

A mysterious Roman bust dating from between the 1st century BCE and the 1st century CE may represent the head of the deceased or an enemy killed in battle. Nearby, look for the small bronze statuette of Isis-Fortuna dating from the 2nd century CE.

The Middle Ages

Exhibits from the Middle Ages include local funerary stele (stone grave markers) in the typical local style. Don't miss the recovered fragments of a 12m-long oak boat, built in Bilbao in the 15th century.

PLANNING TIP
Scan the QR code at the ticket desk for an audio guide, available in English, French, Spanish and Basque. Exhibits are labelled in Spanish and Basque.

Scan for practical information and self-guided audio tours.

WALKING TOUR

Walk the Casco Viejo

The Casco's narrow, pedestrianised streets are best explored on foot. At the heart of Casco Viejo are Bilbao's original seven streets: Barrenkale Barrena, Barrenkale, Carnicería Vieja, Belostikale, Tendería, Artekale and Somera. They date from the 1400s and once formed the city's commercial centre and port.

START	END	LENGTH
Mercado de la Ribera	Teatro Arriaga	1.1km; one hour

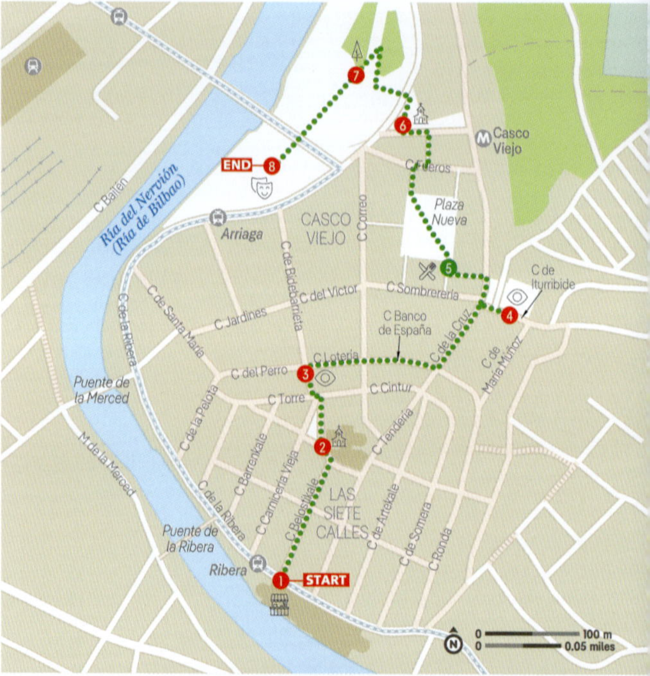

1 Riverside Pintxos

Overlooking the river, the art deco **Mercado de la Ribera** occupies a historic spot, where Bilbao's original seven streets reach the water's edge. This expansive food market is where many of the city's chefs shop for their morning selection of fresh produce. Don't miss the *pintxo* counters on the 1st floor.

2 Bilbao's Oldest Church

Stroll up Calle Belosticalle (Belostikale) to reach the **Catedral de Santiago**, which has a Gothic Revival facade. The cathedral dates from the 14th century, though the Renaissance portico was added in 1571. Above the main entrance, look for scallop shells, symbols of Santiago (St James) and a reference for pilgrims on the northern route of the Camino de Santiago.

3 Historic Water Fountain

Walk clockwise around the cathedral exterior and turn down Calle Bidebarrieta. At the corner of Calle del Perro, fill your water bottle at the **Fuente del Perro**. Dating from 1800, this neoclassical fountain is located at a natural spring where market animals used to drink. Its three taps protrude from lion heads that more closely resemble *perros* (dogs).

4 Poet's Square

Stroll two blocks east and one block north to reach **Plaza Miguel de Unamuno**. Named for local poet and essayist Miguel de Unamuno, this square is where many nights out in the Casco begin. The steps are a popular meeting place.

5 Pintxo Bars

Walk down Libertad alley to reach the iconic blue facade of **Cafe-Bar Bilbao** on the corner of the 19th-century arcaded Plaza Nueva. Here you can take your pick of *pintxo* bars.

6 Baroque Church

Make your way across Plaza Nueva, ducking out at the northwestern corner. Head two blocks north to see the baroque facade of **Iglesia San Nicolás de Bari**.

7 Leafy Plaza

Next, stop for a break in the shade of the tall lime trees of **Arenal**. Don't miss the striking Arenal Kiosk, an art deco bandstand that is sometimes used for concerts.

8 Neobaroque Architecture

Finish at the riverside Plaza de Arriaga, where you can admire the neobaroque facade of **Teatro Arriaga**, built in 1890.

EXPERIENCES

Shop & Snack at Mercado de la Ribera

MARKET

MAP: 1 P36 C5

At the southern edge of the Casco Viejo is **Mercado de la Ribera** (mercadodelaribera.biz), a vast fresh produce market open every day but Sunday. A market has stood at this site since the 14th century, and the current art deco building dates from 1929, except it was completely remodelled in 2013.

If you plan to cook, the market is a fun place to shop for local ingredients. Fishmongers sell freshly caught cod, hake and seafood, and stalls sell meat, fruit, vegetables and dairy products. You can even find a dedicated mushroom stall selling a selection of foraged and cultivated varieties.

If you'd prefer to graze than shop, head to the 1st-floor *pintxo* bars for drinks and snacks. Try a skewer of garlic prawns or a *gilda* (skewer of olives and anchovies). Take your beer and snack to the sunny riverside terrace.

Tour Backstage at Teatro Arriaga

THEATRE

MAP: 2 P36 B3

Sitting in its own plaza by the river, Bilbao's 1200-seat **Teatro Arriaga** (teatroarriaga.eus) hosts a variety of concerts, musicals, plays and dance performances.

Guided 50-minute backstage tours (adult/child €5/free) in English, Spanish and Basque are offered on weekend mornings. During the tour, you'll see a collection of opera gowns, the red velvet and gilded mirrors of the Orient Express room (designed in the style of the train), and the theatre stalls.

In August, the festival of **Aste Nagusia** – a nine-day extravaganza of concerts, traditional Basque sports, parades and fireworks – begins with the appearance of Marijaia (a large puppet) on the theatre's balcony.

Visit the Virgin of Begoña

BASILICA

MAP: 3 P36 D3

Overlooking the Casco Viejo, a 16th-century basilica is located at the site of an apparition of the Virgin of Begoña, the patron saint of Biscay known locally as Amatxu (Mother). She is particularly venerated by Bilbao's seafarers.

From Plaza Unamuno, take the elevator or climb the steps to **Parque Etxebarria** (p41) and walk three blocks east to reach the **Basilica de la Virgen de Begoña** (begona.org; free). The austere Gothic-style vaulted interior is brightened by a gold altarpiece, which contains the statue of the Virgin. Near the entrance hangs a painting of a procession carrying the Virgin to Bilbao during the 1855 cholera epidemic. Allow an hour for the stroll from Plaza Unamuno and back, including time at the basilica.

On 11 October, the **Día de la Virgen de Begoña**, look out for *txikiteros*, groups of friends donning *txapela* (Basque berets) that gather in Plaza Nueva to drink and sing traditional Basque songs in honour of the Virgin.

Bar Crawl in Plaza Nueva PLAZA

MAP: 4 P36 **C3**

The 19th-century arcaded **Plaza Nueva** (Plaza Barria) is home to some of the city's best and most iconic *pintxo* bars. The plaza is popular with locals, who often prefer to have one *pintxo* in each bar before moving on to the next place. *Pintxos* are lined up behind each of the bars – ask for any that take your fancy – but also look for lists of *pintxos* that are made to order, usually written on a board behind the bar.

The square is often full of children playing as their parents keep an eye out from the bars. On Sunday mornings, kids gather to barter over Panini football cards.

The building with the clock, inscribed with the word 'Euskaltzaindia', is the Basque language academy, where the grammatical rules and vocabulary of standardised Euskara batua are determined.

MUSEUM OF BASQUE CULTURE

MAP: 5 P36 **D4**

It's worth checking whether the **Euskal Museoa** (euskalmuseoa.eus), a museum dedicated to Basque history and culture, has reopened. At research time, the museum was closed for renovations with no set reopening. The museum collection includes Basque clothing, looms, fishing nets, model boats, woodcutters' axes, sheep bells and navigational instruments, as well as round funerary stones related to Basque rituals and beliefs. Look to see whether the photographs of Eulalia Abaitua Allende-Salazar are on display. Her black-and-white images of fishmongers, pastoral families and dockworkers capture early 20th-century Basque life.

Admire the Views from Parque Etxebarria PARK

MAP: 6 P36 **D1**

The landmark brick chimney standing tall at the top of the park is a clue that **Parque Etxebarria** occupies a former industrial site, which was once a steel foundry. Covering a hillside between Casco Viejo and the neighbourhood of Uribarri, the park offers fabulous views of the city. Paths and steps lead to the top of the hill, or you can take the lift up from Plaza Unamuno. The park is popular with dog walkers and joggers and is a good place to experience local life.

During the summer festival of Aste Nagusia, the park has fairground rides, food stalls and firework displays.

Browse the Stalls at the Arenal Saturday Farmers Market MARKET

MAP: 7 P36 C2

On Saturdays from 10am to 2.30pm, the area on the east bank of the river known as the **Arenal** is the location of the **Gure Lurreko Merkatua** farmers market. Stop by to buy fresh local produce directly from the growers and makers, including seasonal fruit and vegetables, honey, *txakoli* white wine, sausage and cheese. It's also a good place to buy flowers and plants.

Look out for other seasonal markets here, including book fairs and Christmas market stalls. During festivals, temporary bars called *txosnas* are set up along the Arenal.

Attend a Candlelit Concert at Iglesia de la Encarnación CHURCH

MAP: 8 P36 D6

Just south of Casco Viejo is Atxuri, a neighbourhood with a strong sense of community. The 16th-century **Iglesia de la Encarnación** regularly hosts candlelit concerts, ranging from classical recitals to tributes to bands like Abba and Queen.

It also has a **religious art museum** (eleizmuseoa.com; adult/child €3/free), accessed via the cloister of the attached 16th-century convent.

Grab a Drink at Muelle de Marzana WATERFRONT

MAP: 9 P36 B5

On summer evenings, **Muelle de Marzana**, the riverside quay in Bilbao la Vieja between Puente de la Ribera and Puente San Antón, is one of the best spots in the city for a drink. Take your pick of bars (p45) and enjoy a drink outside.

Explore the Arts Scene in Bilbao la Vieja ART

MAP: 10 P36 B5

The area of Bilbao la Vieja is home to an alternative arts scene and interesting street art. Pieces include **Supervivientes de la Violencia Machista** (Survivors of

THE BASQUE CROSS

A visible symbol of Basque culture is the lauburu, or Basque cross. Lauburu means 'four heads' in Basque, and the cross is named for the four comma-like heads. The meaning of this symbol is debated. Some say it represents the sun, while others claim it represents spirit, life, consciousness and form. It's also used to signify life and death, and so it's found on headstones. Another theory is that it originally appeared on 16th-century tombstones to indicate the grave of a healer of animals and souls (similar to a spiritual healer).

Male Chauvinist Violence), which depicts female solidarity. Look for it at the **Muelle de la Merced** riverside quay between Puente la Ribera and Puente la Merced.

Find several murals at **Plaza de los Tres Pilares** (MAP: 11 P36 **B6**), near Puente San Antón, including a large-scale, brightly coloured piece by Barcelona artist Sixe Paredes, and *Pinturas Negras Bilbao 2015*, a series of black figures painted by SUS033.

To see the work of local artists, check out the latest exhibition at **Okela** (okela.org; MAP: 12 P36 **B5**), a space for Basque contemporary art, including installations and performance pieces.

Nearby, **Desio Artspace** (desioartspace.com; MAP: 13 P36 **A4**) hosts worthwhile exhibitions that can be viewed on Thursday and Friday evenings. The space is also used for painting classes and other workshops.

View Artistic Fakes at the Museum of Reproductions

MUSEUM

MAP: 14 P36 **A5**

Housed in a former church on Calle San Francisco, the **Museo Reproducciones Bilbao** (bilbokoberreginenmuseoa.eus; adult/child €3/free) displays a collection of reproductions of some of the world's finest sculptures. Pieces include exact replicas of the *Niké of Samothrace, Venus de Milo, Diana of Versailles* and Michelangelo's *Moses*. Most of the reproductions were made in the 1930s and '40s.

The museum also hosts temporary exhibitions of work by local artists.

Walk the Paseo de Los Caños

WALKING

MAP: 15 P36 **C6**

This popular riverside walk extends 2km south along the eastern bank of the Nervión, from the neighbourhood of Atxuri to Puente de la Peña. To reach the start of the **Paseo de Los Caños** path from Atxuri train station, walk south along Calle Atxuri for 350m and look for the paved riverside path on the right (just beyond a children's playground).

The *caños* are more than 400-year-old aqueduct pipes created to supply Casco Viejo with fresh water. The pipes were concealed under sandstone slabs, creating a paved path that became known as the Paseo de los Caños.

The path passes underneath the soaring arch of Puente de Miraflores to reach the shallow waters by **Parque Ibaieder** (reached via a footbridge; MAP: 16 P36 **C6**), with ping-pong tables, running circuits and a wooden viewing platform looking out over the water and the hills beyond.

LISTINGS

See p36 for map of locations

Best Places for...

€ Budget €€ Midrange €€€ Top End

Eating

Pintxo Bars

Bacaicoa €
17 D3
At Plaza Unamuno, this bar specialises in various mushroom *pintxos*, cooked to order. *11am-10.30pm Mon-Sat, to 3.30pm Sun*

Baster €
18 C4
Serves a selection of delectable *pintxos*, including octopus skewers, mini quiches and house-made croquettes. *9.30am-10pm Mon-Thu, to 11pm Fri & Sat, to 4pm Sun; basterbilbao.wordpress.com*

Irrintzi €
19 B4
Feast on tasty morsels such as crab and lemon croquettes. Vegetarian and gluten-free options are available. *9.30am-3pm & 7-10.30pm Mon-Fri, 11.30am-11.30pm Sat, noon-4pm Sun; irrintzi.es*

Taberna Basaras €
20 B4
This traditional *taberna* (tavern) is known for its anchovy *pintxos* and excellent wine cellar. *11.30am-4pm & 7-11.30pm Wed-Fri, from noon Sat, noon-4.30pm Sun*

Pintxos Around Plaza Nueva

Cafe-Bar Bilbao €
21 C3
The blue exterior and colourful wall tiles of this *pintxo* bar are emblematic of the city. *7am-11pm Mon-Fri, 8.30am-10.30pm Sat, to 3pm Sun; bilbao-cafebar.com*

Gure Toki €
22 C3
Many consider the *pintxos* here to be Bilbao's best. Look for the mini pastry parcels filled with stir-fried veg and prawns. *9am-11.30pm Mon, Tue & Thu-Sat, 9.30am-4pm Sun; guretoki.com*

Sorgínzulo €
23 C3
This *pintxo* bar has a strong local following. Standouts include calamari and *bacalao al pil-pil* (cod in a creamy sauce). *9.30am-10.30pm; sorginzulo.com*

Bar Charly €
24 C3
Snack on *pintxos* like brie with jam and walnuts, or spinach and goat's cheese croquettes. *10am-11pm*

In Casco Viejo

Casa Victor Montes €€€
25 C3
The 1849-built Victor Montes offers an exquisite interior, an extensive wine list, superb Basque food and a *pintxo* bar. *1-10pm; victormontes.com*

El Txoko Berria €€
26 C4
A great place to try good-value regional dishes, such as pork cooked in rioja wine and prepared in several ways. *1-10pm; eltxokoberria.com*

Los Fueros €€
27 C3
Authentic bistro specialising in Basque seafood, with a contemporary interior and tiled

walls. *12.30-3.30pm & 7.45-10.30pm Wed-Sun; losfueros.com*

Ola Martín Berasategui €€€

28 B4

At Tayko Hotel, this Michelin-starred restaurant serves multicourse tasting menus designed to scintillate the senses. *1.30-3pm Wed, 8.30-10pm Thu-Sun; taykohotels.com*

In Bilbao la Vieja

Agape Restaurante €€

29 A4

Popular modern Basque restaurant offers a good-value daily lunch menu and pricier evening meals. *1.30-4pm Mon-Thu, 1.30-4pm & 9-11pm Fri & Sat; restauranteagape.com*

Perro Chico €€

30 B5

This Marzana restaurant and bar serves Southeast Asian dishes as well as an excellent selection of craft beers. *7.30-10.30pm Mon-Thu, 1-4pm & 8-11pm Fri & Sat, to 10.30pm Sun; perrochicobar.com*

Al Margen €€

31 C6

Impeccably presented contemporary Basque dishes served in a chic riverside dining room. *1.30-3.30pm Tue & Sun, 9-10.30pm Thu-Sat; restaurantealmargen.com*

Mina Restaurante €€€

32 B5

Expect serious culinary creativity on the tasting menu at this riverside restaurant, which some critics call Bilbao's best. *2-3pm & 9-10pm; restaurantemina.es*

Burgers & Tacos

Surfin' Tacos €

33 B4

Head here for nachos, tacos and quesadillas, including several vegetarian options. *1-11pm Sun-Wed, to midnight Thu, 1pm-12.30am Fri & Sat; surfintacos.mx*

GOSE Smash Burgers €€

34 C4

Casco Viejo burger joint serving smashed patties (made by 'smashing' minced beef onto the grill) and fries. Vegan option available. *1-4pm & 7.30-11pm Tue-Sun; goseburger.com*

Txokomex Kantina €€

35 B4

Colourful Mexican restaurant serving fajitas, burritos and tacos made with hand-rolled tortillas. *1-4.30pm & 7-11.30pm Tue-Fri, 1-4.30pm & 8pm-midnight Sat, 1-4.30pm & 8-11pm Sun; txokomex.com*

Ice Cream

Adelia Iváñez €

36 C3

Run by the same family for six generations, it specialises in nougat and nougat-flavoured ice cream. *9am-9pm Mon-Thu, to 10pm Fri & Sat; adeliaivanez.com*

Gelati Gelati €

37 C4

Local chain serving Italian-style gelato and sorbets. Ice-cream flavours include organic strawberry, pomegranate and mango. *12.30pm-midnight; gelatigelati.com*

Drinking

Casco Viejo Cafes

Charamel Gozotegia

38 B4

Sip tea or hot chocolate and sink your teeth into Bilbao's best cinnamon buns, chocolate croissants and *palmeras* (flaky, heart-shaped pastries), baked on site. *8.30am-8pm Mon-Fri, 9am-8.30pm Sat, to 2.30pm Sun*

Bohemian Lane

39 B5

This cosy coffee shop sells coffee, tea and fresh juices, as well as a selection of vegan pastries, cookies and cakes. *9.30am-2pm & 4-8pm Mon-Sat; bohemian lanebilbao.com*

Opila
40 C1
A short stroll north of Casco Viejo, Opila sells a selection of bread and pastries, baked in-house, plus hot chocolate and lots of teas. *8am-10pm*

Barista's Club
41 C4
This coffee shop is a safe bet for a well-made flat white, as well as smoothies, brunch and waffles. *8am-8pm Mon-Sat, 8.30am-3.30pm Sun; atbaristasbilbao.com*

Bilbao la Vieja Bars

Cafe Nervión
42 A4
Corner bar overlooking the River Nervión, serves a range of tasty sandwiches. *10.30am-midnight Sun-Wed, to 1.30am Thu-Sat; cafenervion.com*

Bar Marzana
43 B5
The cosy interior of this riverside bar fills up quickly, but you can take your drinks out to the patio above the estuary. *5-11pm Mon-Thu, to midnight Fri, noon-midnight Sat, to 11pm Sun*

Peso Neto
44 B5
For a laid-back drinking scene, this bohemian spot is hard to top. Stop by for a cocktail and culinary temptations. *11am-1am; pesoneto.es*

Bihotz Cafe
45 B5
This specialty coffee and craft beer house also displays the work of local artists. *4-10pm Tue-Thu, 1-11pm Fri, from 11am Sat, 11am-10pm Sun*

Live Music & DJs

Shelter
46 D4
A small venue with a dance floor. DJ sets and live bands cover the full musical gamut. *9pm-1am Wed, Thu & Sun, to 2am Fri, 5pm-2.20am Sat*

Kabaret
47 B4
DJs keep the party going into the small hours. *midnight-4.30am Thu, to 6am Fri, 6.30pm-6am Sat, to 4.30am Sun Sep-Jun; midnight-4.30am Sun-Thu Jul & Aug*

Hells Bells Rock Pub
48 B4
Plastered with posters, guitars and memorabilia, Hells Bells blasts out tracks from bands such as AC/DC, Mötley Crüe and Metallica. *8pm-2.30am Thu, to 4am Fri & Sat*

Bilborock
49 A4
Set in a 17th-century former church with a ceiling dome, this multipurpose venue is best known for its rock, metal and pop-rock concerts. *hours vary; bilbaogazte .bilbao.eus/bilborock*

LGBTIQ+ Nightlife

El Balcón de la Lola
50 A4
One of Bilbao's most popular mixed LGBTIQ/straight clubs, this place doesn't get going until late. The music is mostly electronic. *1-6am Fri & Sat*

Bizitza
51 B4
This LGBTIQ-friendly Casco Viejo bar is known for its delectable Basque cheesecake. *2pm-1.30am Mon-Thu, to 3am Fri, 2pm-1am Sat, 3-11pm Sun*

Manolita la Primera
52 B5
On Calle Barrenkale, this LGBTIQ+ bar runs themed nights, including drag shows and neon parties. *8pm-1.30am Thu, to 3am Fri & Sat*

La Sinsorga
53 D3
This feminist enterprise is a combined cafe,

shop and events space. *10am-10pm Sun-Thu, to midnight Fri & Sat; lasinsorga.com*

Shopping

Food

La Quesaría

54 C4

Wonderful cheese shop, selling a range of artisan cheeses and other local produce, including Basque craft beers. *10.30am-2pm & 5-8pm Mon-Sat; laqueseriabilbao.com*

Le Chocolat

55 D3

Treats include Bilbao pavement tile chocolates. At Christmas, look for *turrón de sokonusko* (layered nougat). *10.30am-2pm & 5-8pm Mon-Sat; lechocolat.es*

Fashion

Ramón Ezkerra

56 C4

Local designer creates handcrafted women's and men's jackets and other garments, made in Bilbao. *10am-1.30pm & 4.30-8pm Mon-Fri; ramonezkerra.com*

Ätakontu

57 B4

This shop sells the graphic designs of two Bilbao artists. Garments are made locally using organic cotton. *11am-2.30pm & 5-8pm Mon-Sat; atakontu.bigcartel.com*

Supernova Vintage

58 C4

Vintage clothing store for menswear and womenswear from the 1970s through the 2000s. *11am-2pm & 4.30-8pm Mon-Sat; supernovavintageshop.com*

Shoes & Accessories

Libertad Avenue

59 A5

Bilbao designers of handmade sustainable footwear for urban cyclists. *8.30am-2pm Mon-Fri, libertadavenue.com*

Gorostiaga

60 C3

Crafting traditional *txapelas* (Basque berets) since 1857. Styles include flat-topped berets and the oversized *txapeldun*. *10am-1.30pm & 4.30-8pm Mon-Fri, 10am-1.30pm Sat; sombrerosgorostiaga.com*

Art & Books

Magnolia Rare Books

61 C4

As well as secondhand books, this charming shop also sells posters, art prints and vintage photographs. *10.30am-1.30pm & 5.30-7.30pm Mon-Fri; magnoliararebooks.com*

La Ilusa

62 A4

In the San Francisco neighbourhood, this bookshop and gallery has a range of prints and original artworks for sale. *10.30am-2pm & 4.30-8pm Mon-Sat; lailusalibre.com*

Elkar Megadenda

63 C4

Basque publications are strongly represented here. It has an excellent map and travel section. *10am-2pm & 4.30-8pm Mon-Sat; elkar.eus*

Souvenirs

Orriak

64 C4

Orriak sells a range of crafts and souvenirs, including ceramic Bilbao tiles, cardboard models of local landmarks, and Basque figurines. *10am-1.30pm & 4.30-7pm Mon-Fri; orriak.com*

Enjabonadas

65 C4

Come to this appealing neighbourhood shop for aromatherapy oils, candles, crystals, and bars of handmade shampoos and soaps priced by weight. *11am-2pm & 5-8pm Tue-Fri, 11am-2pm Sat; enjabonadas.com*

See p64
for eating, drinking and shopping listings

Explore Bilbao New Town

Outstanding restaurants and cutting-edge architecture define Bilbao's newer neighbourhoods. The city's landmark building, the Guggenheim, has played a key role in transforming Bilbao into the energetic creative hub it is today. For many travellers, this extraordinary art museum is the primary reason for visiting the city. Today, the Frank Gehry–designed Guggenheim stands among other contemporary designs, like the nearby Zubizuri, a bridge designed by Santiago Calatrava, and the Azkuna Zentroa cultural centre. Parks and plazas dot the city centre, and riverside promenades give fine views. The heights of Artxanda offer an even more impressive panoramic sweep of the city.

Getting Around

Walk

Bilbao is easy to navigate and pleasant to explore on foot. It's a 10-minute walk from the Museo Guggenheim Bilbao to the city centre.

Metro

Metro stations include Moyúa, right in the centre of town; Abando for shopping; and San Mamés for the football station and the Intermodal bus station.

Tram

The tram runs along the length of the river, with stops close to the Museo Guggenheim Bilbao, Estadio San Mamés and the Intermodal bus station.

THE BEST

ART MUSEO Guggenheim Bilbao (p52)

PINTXO BAR La Viña del Ensanche (p64)

CITY VIEWS Funicular de Artxanda (p60)

SPORTING EXPERIENCE Athletic Club (p55)

BASQUE DESIGN SHOP DendAZ (p67)

Parque Doña Casilda de Iturrizar (p63)

A
B
C
D
1
2
3
4
5
6
0
500 m
0.25 miles
Av Madariaga
Ría del Nervión
(Ría de Bilbao)
Pedro Arrupe Footbridge
Av Abandoibarra
Guggenheim
Abandoibarra
C Evaristo Churruca
16
15
Bilbobentura
4
Euskalduna
7
Palace
Euskalduna
6
Itsasmuseum
C Lehendakari Leizaola
Alameda Mazarredo
Plaza del Museo
40
Parque de Doña Casilda de Iturrizar
13
Museo de Bellas Artes
5
Parque de la Misericordia
Museo Athletic Club
Athletic Club
Estadio San Mamés
Gran Vía de Don Diego
C de Elcano
63
C de Rodríguez Arias
C Máximo Aguirre
C de Iparraguirre
Sabino Arana
31
Plaza de Campuzano
53
C de Licenciado Poza
19
San Mamés
47
20
21
C de Ercilla
62
54
Alameda de Urquijo
Alameda de Recalde
45
Indautxu
Plaza Arriquibar
Plaza de Indautxu
Alameda de Urquijo
C de Luis Briñas
Av de Sabino Arana
C de María Díaz de Haro
Alameda Doctor Areilza
C Manuel Allende
44
61
Azkuna Zentroa
3
26
C de Gregorio de la Revilla
Plaza de Echaniz
C de Iparraguirre
Alameda de San Mamés
La Casilla
Plaza de la Casilla
Av de la Autonomía
C General Salazar
For more see
Top Experiences p52
Experiences p60
Eating p64
Drinking p65
Shopping p67

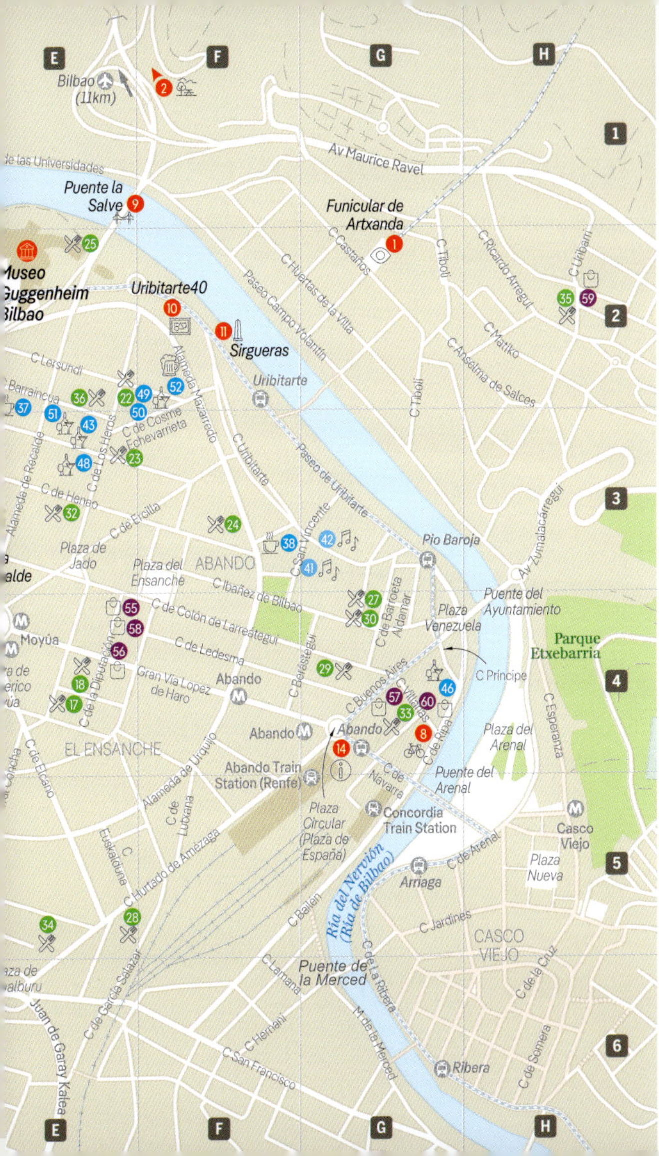
Bilbao (11km)
Puente la Salve
Museo Guggenheim Bilbao
Uribitarte40
Sirgueras
Uribitarte
Funicular de Artxanda
Av Maurice Ravel
C Castaños
C Huertas de la Villa
Paseo Campo Volantín
C Tiboli
C Ricardo Arregui
C Uribarri
C Matiko
C Anselma de Salces
C Lersundi
C Barraincua
Alameda Mazarredo
C de Cosme Echevarrieta
C de Los Heros
Alameda de Recalde
C de Henao
C de Ercilla
C Uribitarte
Paseo de Uribitarte
C San Vicente
Av Zumalacárregui
Pio Baroja
Plaza de Jado
Plaza del Ensanche
ABANDO
C Ibañez de Bilbao
C de Colón de Larreátegui
C de Ledesma
C de Barroeta Aldamar
Plaza Venezuela
Puente del Ayuntamiento
Parque Etxebarria
C Príncipe
Moyúa
Gran Vía Lopez de Haro
C de la Diputación
C Berástegui
Abando
C Buenos Aires
C Villarías
C de Ripa
C Esperanza
Plaza del Arenal
Puente del Arenal
EL ENSANCHE
C de Elcano
Alameda de Urquijo
Abando Train Station (Renfe)
C de Navarra
Concordia Train Station
Plaza Circular (Plaza de España)
C de Luxana
Euskalduna
C Hurtado de Amézaga
C Bailén
Ría del Nervión (Ría de Bilbao)
Arriaga
C de Arenal
Casco Viejo
Plaza Nueva
C Jardines
CASCO VIEJO
C de la Cruz
C de Garcia Salazar
C Lamana
Puente de la Merced
C de La Ribera
C Hernani
M de la Merced
C San Francisco
Ribera
C de Somera
Juan de Garay Kalea
E
F
G
H
1
2
3
4
5
6

★ TOP EXPERIENCE

Museo Guggenheim Bilbao

Opened in 1997, the gleaming, titanium-clad Museo Guggenheim Bilbao is the city's most striking building. The museum galleries display cutting-edge temporary exhibitions alongside pieces from the permanent collection, including works by some of the world's best contemporary artists.

MAP P50 **E2**

PLANNING TIP
Prebook tickets online to avoid queues. The museum is closed on Mondays. Several artworks are located outside the museum and can be viewed without paying the admission fee.

Scan this QR code for opening hours and to book tickets.

Galleries

Start your visit to the **Guggenheim** (guggenheim-bilbao.eus; adult/child €18/ free) in the central atrium, a light-filled space in which the interior architecture of the building can be admired. From here, three floors of galleries emerge, linked by staircases, catwalks and lifts. The museum's galleries house pieces from the permanent collection as well as world-class temporary exhibitions. A single admission fee grants access to all the current works.

Light pours into the **atrium gallery** through cliff-like glass windows, designed to provide views of the river and surrounding hills. At one end, Jenny Holzer's *Installation for Bilbao* features nine LED columns of ever-flowing phrases and text fragments in English, Spanish and Basque.

The Matter of Time

On the ground floor, Richard Serra's *The Matter of Time* is made of a series of sculptures designed to be explored by walking through the tall, carefully balanced steel plates. A subjective, individual experience of time and space emerges as the viewer travels through the narrow corridors and spirals, which are arranged in such a way that it is not

NAEBLYS/SHUTTERSTOCK ©

possible to see the endpoint until you arrive.

To experience the piece as Serra intended, allow yourself to explore the sculptures and notice what arises. Afterwards, go to the 1st-floor gallery to look down on the sculptures and the people walking through them from above.

Permanent Collection Highlights

Not all the pieces in the museum's permanent collection are on view at any one time. You can check the museum's website to find out which works are currently on display.

Expect to queue to visit Yayoi Kusama's installation of coloured lights and mirrors. This popular work makes a striking background for snapping selfies. At busy times, it may be necessary to scan a QR code to join a virtual queue.

Don't miss *Rising Sea* by Ghanaian artist El Anatsui. This large-scale, shimmering metallic

QUICK BREAK

Inside the museum building, **Bistró Guggenheim Bilbao** (bistroguggenheimbilbao.com) serves classic Basque dishes in a contemporary dining room with river views.

PHOTOGRAPHING THE GUGGENHEIM
The best spot for photographing the building is from the opposite bank of the river or Puente la Salve bridge. For a bird's-eye perspective, ride the Funicular de Artxanda.

CHANGING LIGHT
Allow time to walk around the building's exterior, observing how the colours change with the light. Don't miss the building at night, when the lighting gives the exterior a golden glow.

work is made from discarded bottle tops stitched together with copper wire. Also, look for pieces by Mark Rothko and Jean-Michel Basquiat's *Man from Naples*.

Among the museum's collection of contemporary sculptures is *How Profound is the Air* by Basque artist Eduardo Chillida. It is sculpted from alabaster, and the rough natural-stone exterior juxtaposes the highly polished interior.

Another highlight is Jeff Koons' stainless steel *Tulips*, a bubbly, colourful form in Christmas bauble-style high gloss that represents a bouquet of giant balloon flowers (more than 2m tall and 5m across). The work belongs to his ambitious *Celebration* series.

Exterior Works

By the river, look for Louise Bourgeois' spider-like *Maman*. Jeff Koons' *Puppy*, a 12m-tall Highland terrier made up of thousands of flowers, is located on the city side of the museum.

Also by the river is Anish Kapoor's work, *Tall Tree & the Eye*. It consists of 73 reflective spheres anchored around three axes, each of which distorts reality as you look into it.

Lying between the glass buttresses of the central atrium and Ría del Nervión outside the museum is *FOG*, an installation by Fujiko Nakaya: a simple pool of water that regularly emits a mist.

Frank Gehry's Masterpiece

Given a site that was then an industrial wasteland of decaying warehouses on the banks of the Ría del Nervión, architect Frank Gehry designed a building with flowing canopies, ship-like shapes and flying fins.

The building's form and Gehry's use of industrial materials reflect Bilbao's historical links to shipbuilding and fishing. The titanium tiles that sheathe most of the building are like giant herring scales.

★ TOP EXPERIENCE

Athletic Club

Joining thousands of football fans to watch Athletic Club play at the Estadio San Mamés is a memorable experience. At the stadium, Museo Athletic Club offers high-tech exhibits and a behind-the-scenes stadium tour including the changing rooms, tunnel and the pitch.

MAP P50 **A3**

Watching a Match

Passions run deep for Bilbao's football team, Athletic Club (athletic-club.eus), one of Spain's most successful. Their stadium, **Estadio San Mamés** (pictured), overlooks the river and has an architectural design that fits perfectly with the style of Bilbao.

For a classic Bilbao experience, join the fans at La Catedrál (as the stadium is known) to watch Athletic play. Find the dates of upcoming games and buy tickets from the club website or at the stadium ticket office. If you can, dress for the match in red and white (the club's colours), or pick up a shirt at the stadium store.

The atmosphere on match days has a distinctly Basque feel. One stadium song includes the phrase '*alirón, alirón*', which dates back to the 19th-century iron mines and English engineers (all iron!). Locals say that Athletic fans recognise good play and applaud the skills of the opposing team, while holding their own team to high standards.

Athletic Club Museum

Even if you can't catch a game, you can see the stadium and learn about the club's history at the **Museo Athletic Club** (sanmames.athletic-club.eus/museo; adult/child €15/5). The museum and

PLANNING TIP
If you're taking the self-guided museum and stadium tour, bring headphones to use with the audio guide, which you scan with your phone.

Scan this QR code for the museum's opening hours, admission prices and to book ahead.

GORDON BELL/SHUTTERSTOCK ©

QUICK BREAK
Inside the Estadio San Mamés, **La Campa de los Ingleses** (lacampadelosingleses.com) is a cheerfull spot offering *pintxos* (Basque tapas), multicourse lunch menus and weekend brunch with views of the pitch.

stadium tour includes an audio guide (available in English), or you can book online in advance to do the same tour with a tour guide; see the website for available tour times. The guide provides information in Spanish, Basque and English, depending on the group, and you can ask questions. Allow about 90 minutes for the full museum and stadium tour.

The high-tech museum displays gear and trophies dating back to the club's origins in 1898. An innovative display portrays more than 100 years of the club's history in the context of the city of Bilbao's evolution and historical world events. Items to look out for include posters from the 1982 World Cup (hosted by Spain) and a model of La Gabarra, a barge used to transport the team along the river to celebrate cup wins. Don't miss the stuffed lion, a symbol of the club.

In the red zone, use the interactive touch-screens to see game highlights going back some 50 years. You can also practise your penalty-taking skills by kicking a soft ball into the goal on an nteractive screen.

Stadium Tour

From the museum, the immersive tour takes you pitchside, where you can see the stadium and smell he immaculately maintained grass. It continues hrough the press room and press conference area.

In the changing rooms, look for the wall plas-ered with religious icons and other good luck charms. Athletic's players have a particularly close bond because the club's policy of signing only Basque players means they have grown up playing ogether in youth teams.

Next, you can go out through the tunnel to the pitch, sit on the bench and then head up to the president's box and VIP area.

Virtual Reality Experience

n addition to the museum and stadium tour, you an tag on an optional 15-minute immersive irtual reality experience, which simulates the ights and sounds of being on the pitch as a player or Athletic.

Athletic Club Merchandise

At the stadium, the San Mamés Store sells Athletic ootball shirts, baby clothes, stuffed lion toys and ll kinds of branded merchandise. If space in your suitcase (or your budget) is tight, look out for ackets of Athletic potato crisps sold in bars and hops across the city.

LA GABARRA

La Gabarra is the barge, which, when Athletic were crowned champions in 1983, carried the triumphant team and their trophy down the river. In April 2024, when Athletic won the Copa del Rey for the first time in 40 years, more than a million fans packed the riverbanks to cheer as La Gabarra sailed past once again.

WALKING TOUR

Walk Bilbao New Town

This stroll around the new town takes in the best of the neighbourhood's cutting-edge architecture, historic buildings and political institutions. The riverside route offers fabulous views of Bilbao's most iconic sights and the green hills beyond, passing art sculptures, crossing bridges, skirting the city's bustling shopping district and walking through pretty parks along the way.

START	END	LENGTH
Ayuntamiento de Bilbao	Concordia Train Station	4.2km; two hours

1 Elaborate City Hall
Admire the grand 19th-century **Ayuntamiento de Bilbao** (City Hall) before making your way towards the river and the Puente de Ayuntamiento.

2 Over the Water
Stroll northwest along the riverside Paseo Campo Volantín and then cross **Zubizuri**, a wave-like pedestrian bridge designed by Santiago Calatrava and completed in 1997.

3 Riverside Art
Continue northwest along the opposite waterfront. Along the way, look for several sculptures, including ***Sirgueras***, of the Bilbao women who once pulled barges, near the Zubizuri bridge. Don't miss Louise Bourgeois' spider-like *Maman* in front of the city's most famous building, the Museo Guggenheim.

4 Ship-like Concert Hall
Soon, you'll see the **Euskalduna Palace** concert venue, designed to resemble a partly constructed ship, referencing the Euskalduna shipyards that were once located at the site.

5 Elegant Park
Leave the riverbank and stroll through the **Parque de Doña Casilda de Iturrizar**, with its shady trees and pretty pagoda. Pass by the Museo de Bellas Artes.

6 Palacial Architecture
Walk down Calle de Elcano to reach **Plaza de Federico Moyúa** in the centre of the New Town. On your right is the early-20th-century Palacio de Chávarri (note that the building's windows are all different). Turn down Gran Vía and look for the elaborate, late 19th-century Biscay Foral Delegation Palace, where the legislative branch of the Biscay government meets.

7 Pintxo Stop
Take a left on Alameda Mazarredo to reach the pretty Jardines de Albia, overlooked by the 16th-century Iglesia San Vicente Mátir. Stop for a *pintxo* in **Cafe Iruña**, which opened in 1903. Note the Moorish-style arches, exquisite tiling, wooden ceilings, frescoes and marble bar in the cafe's interior. Afterwards, continue down to Calle Lopez de Haro.

8 Art Nouveau Train Station
Look for the remarkable art nouveau facade of **Concordia Train Station**, built in 1902. Walk halfway across nearby Puente del Arenal and look back for better views of the station's decorative wrought iron and tiles.

EXPERIENCES

Enjoy the View from the Funicular de Artxanda

FUNICULAR

MAP: 1 P50 G2

Hemmed in by hills and full of standout architecture, Bilbao looks even better from above. Some of the best views are from the top of Artxanda. The **Funicular de Artxanda** (funiculalrartxanda.bilbao.eus; €4.30 round trip) makes the three-minute trip up and down the hill from the Plaza del Funicular, two blocks east of Zubizuri footbridge. At the top is a park with a bubbly red Bilbao sign and panoramic views across the city and to the sea. Trains leave every 15 minutes, so you could do the trip up and back in under an hour.

Alternatively, explore Artxanda on foot along several **hiking trails**. One option is to start at Puente la Salve and climb to **Pikotamendi** (MAP: 2 P50 F1), a hilltop recreational area with picnic tables and views, and then hike back down through the forests of Potongo to Deutso (4km round trip). Several mountain biking trails are also nearby.

Get a Cultural Fix at Azkuna Zentroa

CULTURAL CENTRE

MAP: 3 P50 D5

Also known as the Alhóndiga, **Azkuna Zentroa** (azkunazentroa.eus) is a former wine storage warehouse turned cultural centre that hosts exhibitions, art workshops and other activities.

The architecture is itself a work of art. The ground floor is supported by 43 Phillipe Starck–designed columns which each reflect distinct cultures and events in world history. Also at the site are several cafes and restaurants, as well as a **rooftop bar** (p66).

There are plenty of accessible public spaces, including a library spread over several floors, making the Azkuna Zentroa a good place to spend a few hours catching up on emails. Also at the site is a cinema and a leisure centre with a glass-bottomed **swimming pool** (adult/child €7.45/4.30), visible from the ground-floor atrium below.

Paddle on the River Nervión

KAYAKING

MAP: 4 P50 A2

Life in Bilbao centres on the Ría del Nervión, so what better way to experience the city than to paddle past the sights in a kayak? Located at the docks by Euskalduna bridge, **Bilbobentura** (bilbobentura.com) has single and double kayaks and SUP boards to hire (€15 for two hours in a single kayak). Life jackets, wetsuits, lockers and waterproof bags for your phone and camera are included.

Two hours is enough time to paddle to the San Antón bridge and back. Along the way, you pass the Guggenheim, Ayuntamiento de Bilbao (city hall), Teatro Arriaga, Concordia Train Station and the

Mercado de la Ribera, drifting under seven bridges to reach Puente San Antón. Early evening is a good time to go, when the sun is less intense.

View the Collection at the Museo de Bellas Artes

MUSEUM

MAP: 5 P50 D3

Bilbao's fine art museum, the **Museo de Bellas Artes** (bilbaomuseoa.eus), houses a compelling collection that includes everything from Gothic sculptures to 20th-century pop art. Allow at least an hour to look around; it's closed on Monday.

The museum has three main subcollections: classical art, with works by Murillo, Zurbarán, El Greco, Goya and Van Dyck; contemporary art, featuring pieces by Gauguin, Francis Bacon and Anthony Caro; and Basque art, with sculptures from Jorge Oteiza and Eduardo Chillida and paintings by the likes of Ignacio Zuloaga and Juan de Echevarría. The museum also hosts temporary exhibitions.

At research time, work was underway on an extension to the museum building, designed by architects Luis María Uriarte and Norman Foster (who designed Bilbao's metro). When the museum renovations are complete, the museum may introduce an admission fee.

Understand Bilbao's Maritime History

MUSEUM

MAP: 6 P50 A2

The historical importance of the sea to the Basques is explained through interactive exhibits at **Itsasmuseum** (itsasmuseum.eus; adult/child €7/3.50, free on Tuesday, closed Monday).

Start by watching the 10-minute video for an overview of Bilbao history from the 1300s to the present. Afterwards, wander through the two floors of displays, which show old shipbuilding techniques, harrowing shipwrecks and innovative coastal rescue strategies, pirate threats, and intricate models of vessels from throughout Bilbao's shipbuilding history. Don't miss

BILBAO'S REGENERATION

Bilbao was once an industrial city defined by its iron and steel works and shipbuilding industry, but by the 1980s, the city was polluted, had high unemployment and was in economic decline. However, the 1990s saw the beginning of a remarkable journey of regeneration. Bilbao got a new metro system, and the opening of the **Guggenheim Museum** and **Euskalduna Palace** put the city centre stage in the world of art and culture. The latest area to undergo regeneration is **Zorrotzaurre** (p63). The plan for the ongoing urban development there was designed by the late architect Zaha Hadid.

the full-scale recreation of the 1511 Consulate Barge. *The Skin of Light* audiovisual installation shows the profound changes Bilbao underwent from the mid-1980s to 2010. The museum also hosts temporary exhibitions of maritime-related art or historical seafaring events.

Outside the museum, on the dock, the 60m-high fire-engine-red 'Carola' crane (1957) was used to build ships on the slipways here.

Listen to Live Music at Euskalduna Palace

LIVE MUSIC

MAP: 7 P50 B2

Built in 1999 on the site of the former Euskalduna shipyards, the **Euskalduna Palace** (euskalduna.eus) was designed to resemble a ship under construction, with an unfinished 'hull' that houses the main auditorium. The venue hosts performances by the Bilbao Symphony Orchestra and the Basque Symphony Orchestra, as well as operas, concerts and musicals.

Free one-hour guided tours of the building are offered most Saturdays from June to September in English, Spanish and Basque. Book online in advance. The highlight is the main auditorium, which has a capacity of 2164. Its design, beechwood panels and oak floors enhance the venue's acoustics.

See Bilbao by Bike

CYCLING

MAP: 8 P50 G4

Bilbao's cycle lanes make it a fun city to explore by bike. **Tourné** (tournebilbao.com) offers daily three-hour guided city tours covering the main sights of the old and new towns (per person €43).

If you prefer to explore on your own, you can hire an e-bike (half-/full-day €20/30) and follow one of Tourné's self-guided routes: the 19.5km route along riverside cycle paths to Puerto Viejo (Portu Zaharra) in Getxo via Portugalete, crossing the Puente Colgante, or the 28km route to Muskiz, home to Bilbao's ironworks. Both routes end at stations for the return train or metro trip back to the city centre. Tourné also has cargo bikes (the kids ride up front; half-/full-day €30/40) and baby seats.

Beyond Bilbao, the beautiful Basque Route coastal cycle trail connects Bilbao with Lekeito (113km) via Bermeo and Gernika. Pick up a map at the tourist office.

Check Out the New Town's Street Art & Galleries

ART

MAP: 9 P50 E1

Bilbao's big-name art museums top most visitors' lists of must-see sights, but the city's smaller galleries, street art and public sculptures are also worth a look.

Beneath **Puente la Salve**, on the east bank of the Ría del Nervión, look for the large mural *La llave* (The Key). The two women in conversation represent the importance of dialogue and mutual understanding.

On the other side of the river, pop into **Uribitarte40** (bilbao arte.eus; MAP: 10 P50 **F2**) a gallery space which hosts the work of artists based at the BilbaoArte Foundation studios.

Nearby, the riverbank sculpture **Sirgueras** (MAP: 11 P50 **F2**), by Dora Salazar, depicts the women who once towed barges from the riverbank, using ropes and their own strength.

Finally, check out **Sala Rekalde** (salarekalde.bizkaia.eus; MAP: 12 P50 **E3**), an avant-garde gallery displaying pieces by Basque artists.

Stroll through Parque de Doña Casilda de Iturrizar

PARK

MAP: 13 P50 **C3**

The elegant **Parque de Doña Casilda de Iturrizar** is planted with maples, lindens, cedars, palms and 70 other species of trees. Its centrepiece is the small pond filled with ducks and swans. Wander along tree-lined avenues and botanic gardens, or sit on the lawns or in the shade of the tiled pergola. It's a pleasant spot for a picnic or an ice cream.

Watch Cutting-Edge Theatre at Pabellón Número 6

PERFORMING ARTS

MAP: 15 P50 **A2**

To tap into Bilbao's arts scene, check what's on at **Pabellón Número 6** (pabellon6.org), an experimental space that hosts performances by a local drama company. Theatre pieces are mostly in Spanish and sometimes in Basque, but the space is also used for contemporary dance performances that don't require language skills to enjoy.

Pabellón Número 6 is located in a former warehouse on **Zorrotzaurre**, an island in the river estuary just west of Euskalduna bridge. Once a wasteland of abandoned industrial warehouses, the area is in the midst of a **regeneration project** (p61), with new residential apartment buildings under construction.

Pabellón Número 6 is one of several artistic ventures to emerge on Zorrotzaurre. Another is **La Terminal** (laterminal.eus; MAP: 16 P50 **A2**), a former factory turned arts space that hosts regular events such as flamenco performances and ecstatic dance sessions.

WALKING TOURS

MAP: 14 PG 110 **B5**

Bilbao's main **tourist office** has a wealth of information on the Basque Country. Head here to book a 1½-hour city walking tour (per person €4.50; guides speak English and Spanish), covering either Bilbao's Old Town (10am Saturday and Sunday) or architecture in New Town (noon Saturday and Sunday). It is possible to book both tours for the same day, with a half-hour break in between.

LISTINGS

Best Places for...

See p50 for map of locations

€ Budget €€ Midrange €€€ Top End

Eating

Pintxo Bars

La Viña del Ensanche €
17 E4
Mouthwatering morsels of ham, seared mackerel and crispy asparagus tempura are among the offerings here. *10am-10.30pm Tue-Fri, from 1pm Sat; lavinadelensanche.com*

El Globo €
18 E4
Offers outstanding *pintxos* (labelled in English) that showcase the great bounty of the Basque countryside. *9am-11pm Mon-Thu, to midnight Fri, 11am-midnight Sat; barelglobo.es*

El Huevo Frito €
19 C4
Many *pintxos* at this relaxed bar feature the eponymous fried egg. *10am-4pm Mon, to 11pm Tue-Fri, 10am-midnight Sat*

Gaztandegui €
20 C4
This *pintxo* bar specialises in cheese, offering the best varieties from the Basque Country and across Spain. *noon-midnight Mon-Sat; bargaztandegi.com*

Seafood

El Puertito €
21 C4
This little bar offers a chalkboard menu of Spanish, French, Irish and Portuguese oysters, served simply with a squeeze of lemon. *noon-10pm; elpuertito.es*

Monocromo €€
22 E2
Vermouth bar and restaurant specialising in grilled seafood. Also serves meat and vegetarian dishes, as well as local wines. *1.30-4pm & 8.30-10pm Tue-Sat, 1.30-4pm Sun; monocromobilbao.com*

Fine Dining

Etxanobe €€€
23 E3
Bilbao-born chef Fernando Canales showcases traditional Basque dishes alongside more technically innovative cooking. *1-3pm & 7.30-10pm Wed-Sat & Mon; etxanobe.com*

Zortziko €€€
24 F3
This elegant restaurant offers à la carte dishes and a choice of tasting menus, including a special grill menu for two (€250). *1.30-3pm & 8.30-10.15pm Tue-Sat; zortziko.es*

Nerua Guggenheim Bilbao €€€
25 E2
The Museo Guggenheim's minimalist, modernist restaurant offers a tasting menu and (more affordable) à la carte options. *1-2.30pm Sun, Tue & Wed, 1-2.30pm & 8-9.30pm Thu-Sat; neruaguggenheim bilbao.com*

Yandiola €€€
26 D5
Inside Bilbao's Azkuna Zentroa cultural centre, Yandiola features modern seasonal Basque and Spanish fare. *1-3pm & 8.30-10.30pm Mon-Fri,*

1-3.30pm & 8.30-10.30pm Sat & Sun; yandiola.com

Basque Food

Bascook €€€
27 G4
Occupying a former salt warehouse, this low-lit space with exposed stone walls makes an atmospheric backdrop for high-end cooking. *11am-6pm Sun-Thu, 11am-6pm & 8.30pm-midnight Fri & Sat; bascook.com*

Casa Rufo €€
28 E5
Tucked in the back of a deli and wine shop, Casa Rufo serves dishes like Navarran asparagus and house-smoked duck. *1.30-4pm & 8.30-11pm Mon-Sat, 1.30-4pm Sun; casarufo.com*

Aitor Rauleaga €€€
29 G4
The elegant dining room matches the classic Basque cooking, including traditional flavoursome stews. *1.30-4pm Mon-Wed, 1.30-4pm & 8.30-11pm Thu-Sat; restauranterauleaga.com*

International

Basquery €€
30 G4
Equal parts microbrewery, bakery, bistro and cafe, Basquery specialises in pizzas, burgers and craft beer. *8.30am-5pm Mon, 8.30am-5pm & 7-11pm Tue-Sat; basquery.com*

Colombo €€
31 C4
A stylish restaurant with booth seating and a globally inspired menu featuring burgers and tempura prawns. *1-4pm & 8-11pm Sun-Thu, to 11.30pm Fri & Sat; colombobilbao.com*

Kimtxu €€€
32 E3
Local ingredients are given an Asian twist to create dishes like Korean steak tartare with Idiazabal cheese. *1.30-3.30pm Tue, 1.30-3.30pm & 8.30-10.30pm Wed-Sat; kimtxu.com*

Vegan & Vegetarian

La Camelia €€
33 G4
With outdoor seating and a few tables inside, this vegan restaurant serves quinoa salads, dips, soups and burgers. *1.30-4pm & 8-11pm; lacameliaveganbar.com*

Garibolo €€
34 E5
The house speciality is vegetarian meatballs. Plenty of vegan options are available, plus a good selection of desserts. *1-4pm Sun-Thu, 1-4pm & 8-10.30pm Fri & Sat; garibolo.com*

Pizza

Margherita La Fina €
35 H2
In Uribarri, this pizzeria serves freshly baked thin-crust pies. *7.30-11pm Mon-Thu, to 11.45pm Fri, 1.30-3.30pm & 7.30-11.45pm Sat, to 11pm Sun*

Coppola €€
36 E2
An atmospheric Italian restaurant serving thin-crust pizzas, risotto, fresh pasta and salads. There's live music three or four nights a month. *1-11pm; coppolabilbao.com*

Drinking

Coffee

Arvo Coffee & Plants
37 E2
If you're fussy about coffee, head to this bright cafe that uses high-quality, freshly roasted beans. Good breakfasts too. *9am-4pm; arvobilbao.es*

Cinnamon
38 F3
This self-styled 'coffee lab' serves locally roasted beans, as well as a selection of teas, juices, brunch dishes and cakes. *9am-2pm; facebook.com/cinnamonbilbao*

Cokooncafé

39 E2

Named for Cokoonsuge, a character in Basque mythology, this cafe serves breakfasts, cookies, and cakes. *9am-2pm Tue-Sun; cokooncafe.com*

Nokora Speciality Coffee

40 D2

Choose from a range of beans and preparation methods. If you're unsure, the baristas can help you choose your brew. *8am-5pm Mon-Fri, 10am-3pm Sat; nokora.coffee*

Live Music

Kafe Antzokia

41 G3

Housed in a former cinema, this iconic Bilbao venue hosts concerts and DJ sets. Check the website to see what's on. *hours vary; kafeantzokia.eus*

Back & Stage

42 G3

This nightclub has two spaces, Stage Live and the Back Room, playing DJ sets, pop music and reggaeton. *midnight-5am Thu, to 6.30am Fri & Sat; backandstage.com*

Residence

43 E3

Hosts regular acoustic jam performances, including Irish and Basque folk music, blues and rock. Great place for a whisky too. *3pm-1am Mon-Thu, from 1pm Fri-Sun; residencecafe.com*

Cotton Club

44 C5

Draws a diverse crowd to its DJ nights and regular gigs – mainly jazz, blues and rock. *8pm-5am Thu, midnight-6am Fri & Sat, cottonbilbao.com*

Rooftop & Riverside Bars

La Terraza

45 D4

Sweeping views over Bilbao's skyline extend from the 12th-floor glass-walled rooftop bar at the top of Hotel Ercilla. *noon-midnight Mon-Wed, to 1am Thu-Sun; ercilladebilbao.com*

La Terraza del Yandiola

see **Yandiola**

A cocktail at this rooftop bar at **Azkuna Zentroa** (p60) is the perfect way to start the night. *2-10pm Mon-Thu, to 11pm Fri, 1-11pm Sat, to 9pm Sun; yandiola.com*

Baobab

46 G4

This cosy riverside bar has an excellent array of teas, infusions, beer, wine, vermouth and snacks. *6-11.30pm Mon, from 4pm Tue-Thu, 4pm-1am Fri, from noon Sat & Sun; instagram.com/baobabteteria*

Wine

Cork

47 C4

Behind the bar, blackboards list the extensive selections of whites and reds available by the glass. *noon-4.30pm & 6-11pm Mon-Thu, to 11.30pm Fri & Sat; cork bilbao.com*

Mr Marvelous

48 E3

A friendly bar with a good wine selection. Try the tortilla, the house specialty. *11am-4pm & 7-10pm Tue-Thu, to 11pm Fri, noon-4pm & 7-11pm Sat*

Cocktails

Gin Fizz

49 F2

Back-lit cabinets and contemporary furnishings make this a stylish place for sipping cocktails. *4pm-1am Sun & Tue-Thu, to 2.30am Fri & Sat; gin-fizzbilbaococktail.com*

Tailor Club

50 F3

This low-lit cocktail bar has a small dance floor for partying into the small hours. *5pm-3am Sun & Tue-Thu, to 5am Fri & Sat*

La Mula de Moscú

51 E3

Their signature Moscow mule is just one of an array of drinks and snacks to enjoy. *4pm-1am Mon-Thu, to 2.30am Fri & Sat, 1-9pm Sun; lamula demoscu.com*

Craft Beer

Singular

52 F2

Sells craft beers, including Basque and international brews. Excellent *pintxos* too. *9.30am-11pm Mon-Thu, to 1.30am Fri, 12.30pm-1.30am Sat; singularbar.com*

Penguin Bar

53 C4

Good choice of craft beers on tap, in bottles and cans. *5-11pm Tue-Thu, to 1am Fri & Sat*

Shopping

Food & Drink

Chocolates de Mendaro

54 D4

An old-time chocolate shop filled with handmade pralines, truffles and nougat. *10am-2pm & 4.30-8pm Mon-Fri, 10am-2pm Sat; chocolatesde mendaro.com*

La Oka

55 E4

This high-end deli and food shop sells a range of Basque and Cantabrian produce. *9.15am-9pm Mon-Sat, 10am-3pm Sun; laoka.es*

Arrese

56 E4

The Gran Vía store is one of several branches of this Bilbao patisserie, in business since 1852. Specialities include Gateau Basque (cream-filled pastry pie). *9am-9pm Mon-Sat, 9am-3pm & 5-8.30pm Sun; arrese.biz*

Music, Books & Art

Power Records

57 G4

The broad array of records here has been keeping Bilbao's vinyl lovers happy since the mid-1990s. *10am-2pm & 4.30-8pm Mon-Sat; powerrecordsbilbao.com*

Astarloa

58 E4

This specialist second-hand bookstore is a joy to browse. It also carries antique artworks. *10am-2pm & 4-8pm Mon-Sat; astarloa.es*

Segunda

59 H2

This small gallery sells illustrations and posters by local artists. *5-8pm Thu, 11am-3pm Fri & Sat; segundalibreriagaleria. bigcartel.com*

Fashion & Design

Persuade

60 G4

A former warehouse with cast-iron columns makes an inspiring backdrop for cutting-edge fashion by top international designers. *10.30am-8pm Mon-Sat; persuade.es*

DendAZ

61 D5

Browse artworks and handicrafts by local artists at the Basque design shop at **Azkuna Zentroa** (p60). *10am-8.30pm; dendaz.azkuna zentroa.eus*

De Flores y Floreros

62 D4

One of several nationwide branches of the Spanish brand of handmade women's shoes. Styles include elegant ballet pumps and sandals. *10.30am-2pm & 4.30-8pm Mon-Sat; defloresy floreros.com*

Henry Arroway

63 C3

Bilbao designer Enrique Arroyabe opened his first outerwear store in the city in 1970. *10.30am-2.30pm & 4.30-8pm Mon-Fri, 10.30am-2.30pm & 4-8pm Sat; henryarroway.com*

See p80
for eating, drinking and shopping listings

Explore
Getxo & Portugalete

The coastal district of Getxo has wide-ranging appeal, with beaches, waterfront promenades and seafood restaurants. Getxo is a sprawling municipality comprising five different neighbourhoods. Highlights include the *pintxo* (Basque tapa) bars of Areeta-Las Arenas, the marina and beaches near Neguri, and the old fishing village of Puerto Viejo in Algorta. Keep heading north to reach even more pristine beaches and dramatic clifftop scenery, a wild beauty within easy reach of Bilbao. On the other side of the Nervión from Getxo is Portugalete, where a pretty medieval centre leads down to the waterfront. Linking Getxo and Portugalete is the monumental Puente Colgante transporter bridge.

Getting Around

Metro

From Bilbao, metro trains for Getxo (Line 1 towards Plentzia) and Portugalete (Line 2 towards Kabiezes) leave from the same platform; check the train's destination. Key stations in Getxo are Areeta (for the Puente Colgante and Las Arenas) and Algorta (for Puerto Viejo).

Bicycle

Bike lanes link Bilbao with Portugalete and the coastal neighbourhoods of Getxo. Bikes are permitted on the Puente Colgante.

Lift

A lift runs between Playa de Ereaga and Avenida Algorta.

Portugalete
KAVRAM/SHUTTERSTOCK ©

★ **THE BEST**

PIONEERING DESIGN Puente Colgante (p72)

SEAFOOD Karola Etxea (p80)

AIR-BORNE VIEWS Paragliding flight (p77)

MEDIEVAL TOWN Portugalete (p79)

HILLTOP HIKE Monte Serantes (p79)

PORTUGALETE & AREETA
0 500 m
0 0,25 miles
For more see
Top Experiences p72
Experiences p76
Eating p80
Drinking p81
Shopping p81
Muelle de Arriluce
Galerías de Punta Begoña
Muelle de Ereaga
El Abra Marina
Puerto Deportivo de Getxo
C Marqués de Arriluce e Ibarra
Av Algorta
Palacio Lezama-Leguizamón
Av de Asua
Av Zugatzarte
Casa Cisco
Gobela
Paseo de las Grandes Villas
C Cristobal Valdes
C Lertegi
C Negubide
Muelle de Las Arenas Areeta
Av Zugatzarte
C Ibaiondo
C Kresaltzu
C Ama Mesedeetakoa
C Andres Larrazabal
Playa de Las Arenas
Evaristo Churruca Monument
Peñota
C Bizkaiko Aurrezki Kutxa
C Santa Eugenia
Areeta
C Nagusia
Av Areetako
C Amistad
C Bidebarrieta
Muelle Churruca
C María Díaz de Haro
Muelle Evaristo Churruca
Av Abaro
AREETA
Puente Colgante
C Eduardo Coste
C Amaia
Peñota
PORTUGALETE
C General Castaños
Av Libertador Simón Bolívar
Plaza del Solar
C Santa Ana
Torre de Salazar
Ría del Nervión
Av Autonomía
Basílica de Santa María
Av de Carlos VII
C Gregorio Uzquiano
Rialia Museo de la Industría
Portugalete (Renfe) Train Station
Portugalete

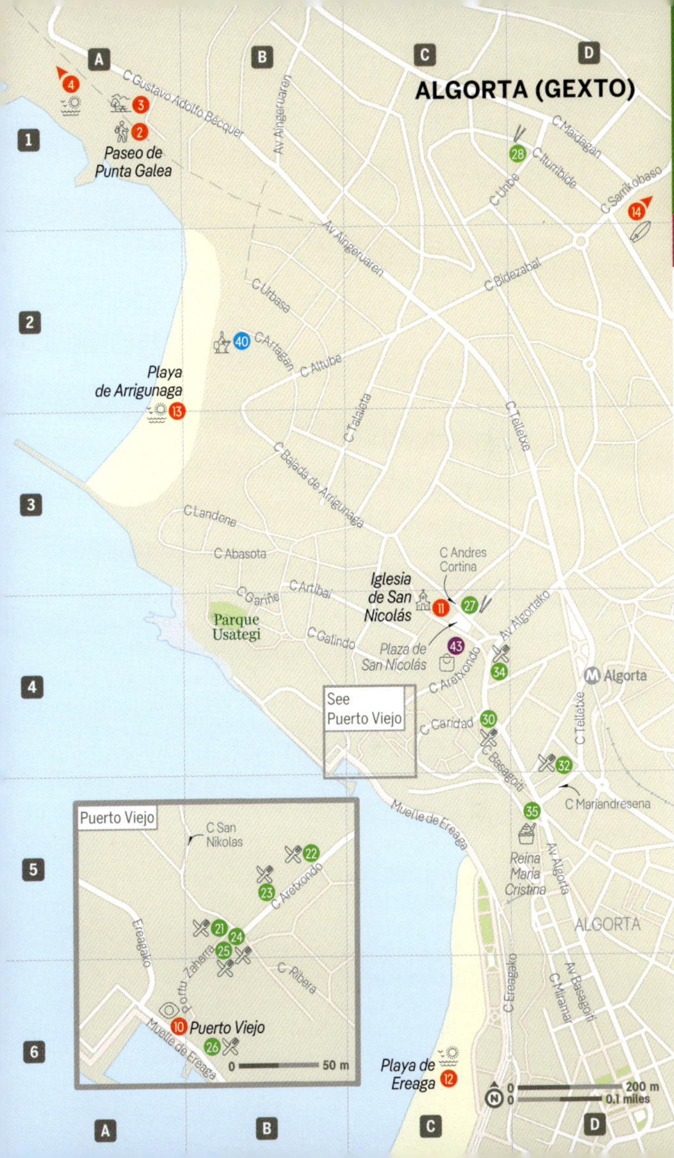
ALGORTA (GEXTO)
C Gustavo Adolfo Bécquer
Paseo de Punta Galea
Av Aingeruaren
C Maidagan
C Iturribide
C Umbe
C Sarrikobaso
C Bidezabal
C Urbasa
C Artagan
C Altube
Playa de Arrigunaga
C Talaiata
C Telletxe
C Bajada de Arrigunaga
C Landene
C Abasota
C Andres Cortina
C Gariñe
C Artibai
Iglesia de San Nicolás
Parque Usategi
C Galindo
Plaza de San Nicolás
Av Algortako
C Aretxondo
Algorta
See Puerto Viejo
C Caridad
C Basagoiti
C Mariandresena
Muelle de Ereaga
Reina Maria Cristina
Av Algorta
ALGORTA
C Ereagako
C Miramar
Av Basagoiti
Playa de Ereaga
Puerto Viejo
C San Nikolas
C Aretxondo
Ereagako
Portu Zaharra
C Ribera
Puerto Viejo
Muelle de Ereaga
0 50 m
0 200 m
0 0.1 miles

★ TOP EXPERIENCE

Puente Colgante

Also known as the Vizcaya or Bizkaia Bridge, the Puente Colgante opened in 1893 and was the world's first transporter bridge. Its suspended carriage carries cars and passengers over the Ría del Nervión. You can also take a windy walk along the top of the structure.

MAP P70 **B5**

PLANNING TIP
Buy tickets to walk across the *pasarela* (catwalk) in the souvenir shops on either side of the bridge. The ticket includes a return trip in the suspended gondola.

Scan this QR code for opening hours and to book tickets.

A Feat of Engineering

The UNESCO World Heritage listed **bridge** (puente-colgante.com), listed in 2006, was designed by Alberto de Palacio, who sought to create a structure that would allow people to cross the river estuary without interrupting the passage of boats to the erstwhile docks, along what was then one of Europe's busiest channels. Palacio's solution was to build a structure tall enough (45m high) to allow ships to pass underneath, with a suspended transporter platform that would glide over the water, carrying passengers between Getxo and Portugalete. Journeys would be timed to avoid clashes with passing boats. The bridge took three years to construct and was a marvel of its day.

Crossing the Pasarela

For a thrilling, up-close experience, take the lift on either side to the *pasarela* that extends for 160m along the top of the bridge (adult/child €10/8). Near the lift on the Las Arenas side, look for the driving engineer's cabin, with the original navigation equipment. Until 1999, this booth was used by the engineer who drove the gondola from above, keeping a lookout for ships.

DVOEVNORE/SHUTTERSTOCK ©

Dare to peer down between wooden planks to the water below as you take the windy walk across. As you cross, look for the red hillside, north of Portugalete; these are the old Somorrosto iron mines. The red paint for the bridge was chosen to reference the colour of this hillside.

On the Portugalete side, walk up to the square to see the bust of Alberto de Palacio looking out to the bridge. It's a good spot for photos. Find another statue of Palacio in Plaza del Puente in Las Arenas.

Riding the Gondola

You can ride between Getxo and Portugalete in the *barquilla*, the suspended gondola that transports pedestrians, cars and bikes. Use the Barik transport card to pay or buy a ticket from the machines on either side of the bridge (foot passengers €0.55; a return ride is included in the gantry walkway ticket price). The trip takes 1½ minutes each way.

QUICK BREAK
Take your *pintxos* and drinks to the outdoor tables on the terrace at **El Puente** (elpuentelasarenas.es), which has unrivalled views of the bridge.

WALKING TOUR

Walk Getxo

A quick metro ride from Bilbao, the seaside district of Getxo offers a serene escape from the city. Clifftop views, pretty beaches and the atmospheric narrow lanes of an old fishing village set the stage for an enchanting afternoon wander. There are also plenty of opportunities for snacking along the way, so come with an appetite.

START	END	LENGTH
Playa Gorrondatxre-Azkorri	Plaza de San Nicolás	9km; 3½ hours

1 Sandy Beach

Head to Azkorri (take bus A3411 from Algorta metro). Walk down to the sandy **Playa Gorrondatxre-Azkorri**. Backed by grassy dunes, it might be Getxo's most beautiful beach, and it's patrolled by lifeguards in summer. Take the path back up to the clifftops to pick up the signed GR-123 coastal trail from just beyond the Azkorri car park towards Areeta.

2 Clifftop Walk

Walk along the clifftops strewn with wildflowers, with views out to the Atlantic Ocean. Continue around the headland, passing a golf course and cemetery, to reach the straight, paved **Paseo de Punta Galea**.

3 Former Windmill

Soon you'll reach **Aixerrota Windmill** (closed to the public), which was built to counter drought-affected watermills and was in operation from 1727 until 1787.

4 Ocean Views

Continue to the ideally located **Ilunabar**. Take your coffee, beer or snack out to the terrace, with views of Playa de Arrigunaga below.

5 Surf Spot

Follow the GR-123 trail over the cliffs, passing **Parque Usategi**. Joggers and dog walkers frequent this small park. It overlooks Jeffrey's Surf Spot, a favourite with local surfers thanks to waves of up to 3m.

6 Old Port

You'll soon reach Puerto Viejo, which feels like a vestige from another era. Steep, narrow lanes skirt past stone cottages decorated with brightly painted shutters and balconies draped with hanging plants. Once the domain of sailors and fisherfolk, the small seaside community remains tightly knit. Stop for drinks and *pintxos* at **Arrantzale Taberna**.

7 Local Square

Walk up Calle Aretxondo to Plaza de San Nicolás, one of the prettiest squares in Getxo. It's also a completely local scene, with a handful of outdoor cafes across from the grand **Iglesia de San Nicolás**. It's liveliest in the afternoons. You might catch locals playing the Basque sport pelota at the square's *frontón* (court).

EXPERIENCES

Learn About Portugalete's Industrial History
MUSEUM

MAP: 1 P70 C6

On the waterfront in Portugalete, just south of the Puente Colgante is the **Rialia Museo de la Industría** (rialia.eus; adult/child €3/free), with displays on the area's industrial history.

Take the lift to the top floor and work your way down through the galleries. Paintings, old photographs, models and machinery parts chart the town's development and the effect early industrialisation had on the area's landscape and social makeup. Best of all are the short films showing fiery industrial action – smelting, welding and molten flows – backed by dramatic musical arrangements.

Ride Along the Water
CYCLING

Getxo's **waterfront cycling path** is great for a spin. One option is the 5km stretch from just south of the Puente Colgante transporter bridge to Algorta's old port area, Puerto Viejo.

You can hire an e-bike using the area's bike-sharing network, **Bizkaibizi** (bizkaibizi.eus), but you need to pay the yearly charge of €25 to sign up. Download the app on your phone to register (it's easy, and the app is available in English) and then scan the QR code to use a bike.

Getxo and Portugalete have plenty of Bizkaibizi stations, including one half a block north of the Puente Colgante, at Areeta metro station, and one near Algorta metro station.

Hike the Clifftop Paseo de Punta Galea
HIKING

MAP: 2 P71 A1

The **Paseo de Punta Galea** is a gentle hiking trail around the cliff-bound promontory that juts into the sea north of Getxo (6km; allow about 1½ hours). The headland is characterised by its exposed rock strata and white cliffs.

Start your walk at the **Aixerrota recreational area** (MAP: 3 P71 A1) on Calle Gustavo Adolfo Bécquer in Getxo (nearest metro Bidezabal). Heading north from here, the Paseo de Punta Galea hugs the clifftops, skirting hedgerows and pine forests. In late spring, butterflies flit between fragrant wildflowers. The path is a prime spot for birdwatching; look out for Sardinian warblers, peregrine falcons and stonechats.

At **Playa de Sopelana** (MAP: 4 P71 D1), you can descend the steep path down to the sand and take a dip in the sea (swimwear optional – the beach is nudist). Look for the lifeguarded swimming area marked by flags. From Sopelana, it's a 15-minute walk to Larrabasterra metro.

Paraglide Along the Coast

PARAGLIDING

On clear days, you'll see paragliders taking flight from near the golf course on **Paseo de Punta Galea** (p76) in Getxo and from the cliffs near **Sopelana beach**. From April to September, you can book a tandem paragliding flight with **Escuela Vasca Parapente** (escuelavascadeparapente.com).

A 20- to 25-minute tandem flight costs €59, including equipment, instruction and insurance (the total activity time is 45 minutes). The minimum age for children is seven years old.

The pilot guides the paragliding flight, which travels at around 35km/h. For many people, the experience of gliding through the air is both relaxing and exhilarating; some feel a rush of joy at the beauty of the scenery and the feeling of flying.

Walk Along Las Arenas Waterfront

HISTORIC BUILDINGS

MAP: 5 P70 C3

In the Getxo neighbourhood of Las Arenas, take a stroll along **Paseo de las Grandes Villas** to see the elaborate mansions that line the waterfront.

The Paseo is the unofficial name given to the seafront area of Muelle de Las Arenas and Muelle de Arriluze. Interpretative panels give details of the mansions along the route, many of which date from the town's heyday in the early 20th century.

Start at the northern end, near the turreted **Palacio Lezama-Leguizamón** (MAP: 6 P70 D1), built in 1902 but revamped by Bilbao architect Manuel María Smith in 1921. Its central tower is based on the Monterrey Palace in Salamanca. As you make your way along the waterfront promenade, look out for the 1911-built **Casa Cisco** (MAP: 7 P70 D2), also by Manuel María Smith.

PELOTA: THE ULTIMATE BASQUE SPORT

Throughout the Basque Country, every town and village has a pelota court, or *frontón*, around which the local community gathers to watch matches. Basques have several traditional sports and games, including log cutting, stone lifting, hay-bale throwing and tug-of-war. But the most popular is pelota, a fast-moving ball game that can be played with small wooden racquets or a *chistera* (a long basket). *Pelota mano* (hand ball) involves players using their bare hands to thwack the ball against the *frontón* wall. In Algorta, look for the *frontón* in Plaza San Nicolás.

The southern end of the seafront is marked by a monument to **Evaristo Churruca** (MAP: 8 P70 B4), a 19th-century engineer who worked on the town harbour. Allow about 30 minutes for the 1.5km stroll.

Look Inside a Landmark at Galerías de Punta Begoña — HISTORIC BUILDING

MAP: 9 P70 C1

The massive stone structure of the **Galerías de Punta Begoña** (puntabegonagetxo.eus) was built in 1919 as a continuation of Getxo's defensive wall. It's an impressive sight, complete with columns and a balustraded terrace, though it's in a bad state of decay. Long-term restoration, however, is underway.

While it's not all open to the public, one-hour guided visits in Basque and Spanish are offered Friday to Sunday (€2; book online in advance).

Stroll Through Puerto Viejo — AREA

MAP: 10 P71 A6

At the northern end of the Playa de Ereaga, **Puerto Viejo** is a warren of steps and narrow alleyways lined with traditional whitewashed fishers' houses, colourful flower pots, bars and seafood restaurants.

In Algorta, stop to take a look at **Iglesia de San Nicolás** (MAP: 11 P71 C4) and the model ship hanging near the organ. At the side of the church is a *frontón*, a court where you might see people playing the traditional Basque sport of pelota.

From Plaza San Nicolás, follow Calle de San Nicolás down to reach Puerto Viejo, where steps and pedestrianised alleyways lead down through the cottages of what was once a fishing village. Take your pick of bars for fresh seafood *pintxos* and a glass of local *txakoli* wine. Just beyond the terrace of **Arrantzale Taberna** (p80), look for statues of a fisherman and a sardine seller, a tribute to Puerto Viejo's past.

Soak Up the Sand & Surf at Getxo's Beaches — BEACH

MAP: 12 P71 C6

Getxo has a number of beaches easily accessed by metro from Bilbao.

In Las Arenas, **Playa de Ereaga** is a long, sheltered sandy beach that runs between the Galerías de Punta Begoña and Puerto Viejo. It's good for families. Beach football tournaments take place here in summer.

Further north, near the mouth of the Nervión estuary, **Playa de Arrigunaga** (MAP: 13 P71 A3) is a lovely stretch of beachfront backed by a steep hillside. It's a great spot to slow down and take in the scene, with skaters zipping around at a skate park near the centre of the beach and surfers out on the waves.

An even better spot for surfing is **Playa de Sopelana** (p76).

Several places rent surf gear and offer lessons, including **Peña Txuri Surf School** (escueladesurfsopelana.com; MAP: 14 P71 D2).

Explore Portugalete's Medieval Sites

HISTORIC BUILDINGS

MAP: 15 P70 B6

Portugalete's medieval lanes lead down to a serene waterfront square. Allow an hour or two to stroll the streets, snap photos of the bridge and estuary, and stop for a drink.

Start at the top of the town at the 15th-century **Basílica de Santa María** (iglesiasdebizkaia.com), which stands atop an earlier 14th-century church that once marked the town's highest point. The striking structure is largely Gothic, with flying buttresses, gargoyles and austere sandstone walls. The bell tower was a later 18th-century addition. Inside, don't miss the carved wood Renaissance-era altarpiece.

Next, take a look at the stubby four-storey **Torre de Salazar** (MAP: 16 P70 B6), originally part of a defensive complex built by the local Salazar family in the 15th century.

Make your way down to the cobbled **Plaza del Solar** (MAP: 17 P70 B6), a picturesque spot with 19th-century buildings and a monument to Víctor Chávarri (1854–1900), a local industrialist and politician. At the plaza's heart is an ornate bandstand.

SET SAIL

MAP: 18 P70 C1

Getxo is a hot spot for sailboat cruises around the bay. Several operators are based in the **Puerto Deportivo de Getxo** (pdgetxo.eus) in Las Arenas. **Marmitako** (marmitakosailing.com) offers full- and half-day scenic sailboat tours, as well as sunset tours with cocktails and snacks.

Take in the Views From Monte Serantes

HIKING

MAP: 19 P70 A5

Stage 15 of the long-distance GR123 hiking trail is the 21.8km waymarked route from Portugalete to Muskiz (allow about seven hours). The highlight of the hike is the trail up **Monte Serantes** (451m), which can be done as a shorter walk (11km round-trip) from Santurtzi metro, 2km north of Portugalete. Allow three to four hours.

The trail passes the ruins of **Serantes Fort** (1882; MAP: 20 P70 A5), painted with a mural representing nature and Basque mythology, as well as birdwatching hides. Best of all is the magnificent view over Bilbao.

LISTINGS

Best Places for...

See pp70-71 for map of locations

€ Budget €€ Midrange €€€ Top End

Eating

Around Puerto Viejo

Arrantzale Gastrotaberna €€
21 P71 B5
This upstairs bistro restaurant serves local fare, such as mussels cooked in *txakoli* wine. *1.30-3.30pm & 8-10pm Tue-Sun, 1.30-3.30pm Sun; arrantzale.com*

Restaurante Goiezti €€€
22 P71 B5
Goiezti specialises in grilled meat and local seafood, including wild sea bass, swordfish and squid. *1-4pm Sun & Tue-Thu, 1-4pm & 9-11pm Fri & Sat; goiezti.es*

Karola Etxea €€€
23 P71 B5
Feast on fresh seafood at this atmospheric Basque restaurant, family-run for three generations. *1.30-3.45pm & 9-11pm; karolaetxea.net*

Pintxos in Puerto Viejo

Txomin Taberna €
24 P71 B5
In the atmospheric lanes of Puerto Viejo, this bar has snacks (croquettes, anchovies, mussels in tomato salsa) and sea views. *noon-midnight*

Arrantzale Taberna €
25 P71 B6
The tree-shaded terrace of this laid-back bar is a top spot to sip wine or beer and nibble on *pintxos* or a plate of chorizo in cider or local Idiazabal cheese. *noon-11pm; arrantzale.com*

Itxas Bide Taberna €
26 P71 B6
This traditional waterfront bar is known for its croquetas. The upstairs restaurant specialises in seafood. *10am-11pm*

Japanese

Nikkou €€
27 P71 C4
For sushi in a contemporary dining room, head to Nikkou on Plaza San Nicolás in the Algorta neighbourhood of Getxo. *12.30-4.30pm & 8-11.30pm Wed-Mon; nikkou.es*

Iwasaki €€€
28 P71 D1
Choose between the Youkoso (€35) and Omakase (€52) menus at chef Tatsuya Iwasaki's restaurant in Algorta. *2-3pm Wed, Thu & Sun, 2-3pm & 8.30-9.30pm Fri & Sat; iwasaki.es*

Burgers & Brunch

Pau Cafe €
29 P70 C4
This Las Arenas cafe serves breakfast, brunch, *pintxos*, smoothies and good coffee. *8am-10pm Mon-Thu, to 11pm Fri, 10am-11pm Sat, to 4pm Sun*

Tellagorri €€
30 P71 C4
Serves burgers and nachos, as well as fries with different cheese and meat toppings. *noon-midnight Sun-Thu, to 2am Fri & Sat; tellagorri.com*

Amaya Burger €
31 P70 D4
Serves gourmet burgers with a range of toppings, including pulled pork and Idiazabal cheese. *1-3.45pm & 7.30-10.45pm Sun-Thu, to 11.45pm Fri & Sat; amayaburger.com*

Lamami Txinuk €

32 P71 **D4**

Choose from 12 craft beers on tap to drink with burgers, tacos and other bar snacks. *noon-4.30pm & 7.30pm-midnight Fri-Mon, 7.30pm-midnight Tue-Thu*

Cakes & Pastries

Pastelerias Zuricalday €

33 P70 **C4**

This traditional bakery and cafe specialises in *bollos de mantequilla*, sweet rolls filled with cream. *9am-2pm & 4.30-8pm Mon-Fri, 9am-2.30pm & 5-8pm Sat, to 3pm Sun; pasteleriaszuricalday.es*

Amasarte Labea €

34 P71 **C4**

A small bakery selling freshly made sourdough loaves as well as pies, pastries and cakes. *9am-2.30pm Tue-Sat*

Ice Cream

Galdaretxe €

35 P71 **D5**

Sells a range of cakes, pastries and breads, as well as delicious ice creams. *8.30am-9pm; galdaretxe.com*

Aberasturi Helados €

36 P70 **C5**

This artisan ice-cream parlour is a Las Arenas institution, founded in 1926. *noon-10pm Mon-Fri, from 11.30am Sat & Sun*

Around Portugalete

Txiki €

37 P70 **B5**

Near the waterfront, Txiki is one of the friendliest places in town for a *cidra* (cider) and *pintxos*. *10.30am-3pm & 5.30-10pm*

Punta Malabata €€

38 P70 **B5**

Punta Malabata serves informal, Asian-fusion-style food (bao buns, hamburgers, stir-fries) and craft beer. *1-4pm & 8-11pm; puntamalabata.es*

El Paladar €€€

39 P70 **B5**

At the Puente Colgante Boutique Hotel, eight- and 12-course tasting menus showcase Basque cuisine. *1.30-3.30pm Sun, Wed & Thu, 1.30-3.30pm & 8-10.30pm Fri & Sat, puentecolganteboutique hotel.com*

Drinking

Around Getxo

Ilunabar

40 P71 **B2**

Ilunabar's glass-sided terrace is a great place for sunset cocktails. *9.30am-11pm*

Embarcadero

41 P70 **C3**

At the Las Arenas waterfront, the bar and terrace of the Hotel Embarcadero are open for morning coffee through to late-night drinks. *8am-1am; hotelembarcadero.com*

Bar Jai Alai

42 P70 **D4**

Modern *pintxo* bar with creative bites, washed down with beer or wine. *7am-10.30pm Mon-Wed, to 11pm Thu, 7am-midnight Fri, from 8am Sat, 8am-10.30pm Sun*

Shopping

Food & Drink

Mimarte

43 P71 **C4**

Sells a range of teas and coffees, stored on shelves in large jars, as well as mugs and teapots. *10.30am-2pm & 5-8.30pm Mon-Fri, 10.30am-2pm Sat; mimarte.shop*

Mundo de Cervezas

44 P70 **D4**

Head here for craft beers from all over the world, including local brews. *10.30am-2pm & 5-8pm Mon-Fri, 10.30am-2pm Sat; mundodecervezas.es*

★ WORTH A TRIP

Gernika

Surrounded by the forested hills and birdsong from the Urdaibai Biosphere Reserve, Gernika is the symbolic centre of Basque culture and politics. Visit the moving Museo de la Paz (Peace Museum), which marks the site of the devastating bombing the town suffered during the Spanish Civil War.

PLANNING TIP
Euskotren trains connect Bilbao with Gernika (45 minutes). Gernika's sights are all within easy walking distance of the train station. Pick up a map at the tourist office.

Scan this QR code to book a free visit to the Gernika Assembly House.

Peace Museum

On 26 April 1937, the town of Gernika suffered sustained bombing attacks by Hitler's Condor Legion and Mussolini's Aviazzione Legionaria, acting on the orders of Franco. In the chaos that followed, no death toll was taken. Based on hospital reports, the Basque government calculated the number of recorded deaths to be 1654.

The **Museo de la Paz** (museodelapaz.org; adult/child €6/free) puts the event in context and uses witness testimonies to recount what happened that day. Most moving is a visual and audio recreation of a local living room at the moment the bomb struck. Picasso depicted the bombing in his 1937 oil painting Guernica, and a tiled **reproduction** of the work can be seen at the corner of Calles Pedro Elejalde and San Juan.

Basque Culture

The historical importance of Gernika far predates the Spanish Civil War. From medieval times until 1876, representatives from Biscay province had meetings under an oak tree known as the Árbol de Gernika. These days, representatives meet once a month in the **Gernika Assembly House** (Casa de Juntas; pictured). When not in session, the

MIKEDOTTA/SHUTTERSTOCK ©

building is open to the public. Admission is free, but you need to book a slot online (jjggbizkaia.eus). Don't miss the stained-glass windows and artwork; scan the QR codes for an audio guide in English. On the grounds, look for the dried trunk of an earlier **Árbol de Gernika** and see the current tree, planted in 2015.

If you have time to spare, check out the displays on Basque sports, folklore and mythology at the **Museo de Euskal Herría** (bizkaikoa.bizkaia.eus; adult/child €6/free).

Lastly, take a walk around the **Parque de los Pueblos de Europa** to view two large sculptures: *Large Figure in a Shelter* by Henry Moore and *Our Father's House* by Eduardo Chillida. The latter forms a window through which the Árbol de Gernika can be seen.

QUICK BREAK
Located right in the centre of town, **Auzokoa** whips up some of the best *pintxos* (Basque tapas) in Gernika, including scallop gratin served on the shell.

See p94 for eating, drinking and shopping listings

Explore Central Basque Coast

The coastline between Bilbao and Donostia-San Sebastián has spectacular scenery, with cove after cove of sun-dappled waves and verdant fields that end where the cliffs plunge into the sea. While some people stop for a day or two along the way, you could easily make a week of it, basking on lovely beaches, walking along the craggy coastline and delving into the history of the place, taking in everything from 100-million-year-old rock formations to a futuristic museum devoted to couture. A particularly beautiful area is the Urdaibai estuary, an important wetland habitat that is a key resting site for migratory birds. The reserve, listed by UNESCO in 1984, comprises some 23,000 hectares of Atlantic coastline, marshes and Cantabrian oak forest.

Getting Around

Train

Euskotren trains connect Bilbao with Mundaka and Bermeo. The San Sebastián to Bilbao Euskotren service stops in Zarautz, Zumaia and Deba.

Bus

The A3512 bus takes the fastest route from Bilbao Intermodal to Lekeitio. For Getaria, take the UK10 bus from San Sebastián bus station.

Car

Driving is the easiest way to reach sites outside the main towns, but coastal roads are busy in summer. The Basque Route cycle trail runs along the coast between Bilbao and Donostia-San Sebastián.

Urdaibai estuary (p92)
JON CHICA/SHUTTERSTOCK ©

★

THE BEST

CLIFFTOP HIKE Deba to Zumaia (p90)

SURF SPOT MUNDAKA (p92)

MUSEUM Cristóbal Balenciaga Museoa (p87)

SEAFOOD RESTAURANT Elkano (p94)

BIRDWATCHING Urdaibai Bird Center (p92)

A
B
C
D
E
F
1
2
3
4
0
20 km
0
10 miles
For more see
Top Experiences p87
Experiences p92
Eating p94
Drinking p95
Shopping p95
San Juan de Gaztelugatxe
Crusoe Treasure
9
8
Doniene Gorrondona
Plentzia
Bermeo
10
Mundaka
Mundaka
1
6
11
Elantxobe
Playa de Laida
Mungia
Urdaibai Bird Center
3
Guernica
Bilbao Airport
Bilbao
Amorebieta
15
Isla de San Nicolás
4
Lekeitio
5
Ondarroa
13
Mutriku
Deba
Elgoibar
Eibar
Flysch Boat Tours
2
Zumaia
Getaria
12
Playa Zarautz
7
14
Zarautz
Cristóbal Balenciaga Museoa
Azpeitia
San Sebastián (15km)

★ TOP EXPERIENCE

Cristóbal Balenciaga Museoa

The aesthetic appeal of the pretty coastal town of Getaria extends beyond its appealing cobblestone lanes to its gleaming fashion museum. Cristóbal Balenciaga Museoa showcases the work of the local designer who became a giant in the fashion world in the 1950s and '60s.

MAP P86 **F3**

Viewing the Collection

The **museum**'s (cristobalbalenciagamuseoa.com; adult/child €13/free) collection of more than 3000 Balenciaga pieces are displayed on themed rotation, and is freshly curated several times a year. Balenciaga's work is displayed alongside pieces by other artists to highlight shared shapes or influences.

The biographical gallery gives an overview of the life of the fashion innovator once viewed as the king of couture. Afterwards, wander through futuristic galleries, where the pieces are artfully lit. Look out for the Infanta gown, inspired by costumes worn by Spanish princesses as painted by Diego Velázquez.

One-hour guided museum tours are offered in Spanish and Basque at weekends.

Workshops & Classes

The museum also offers courses, ranging from haute couture techniques to one-day family fashion-designing and clothes-dying workshops (where you learn to use fruit and vegetables to make natural textile dyes). Check the website for upcoming course dates and prices.

Exploring Getaria

If you like seafood, try the catch-of-the-day in one of Getaria's **restaurants** (p94). Allow two or three hours to wander the town, eat lunch by the port and relax on the beach.

PLANNING TIP
The museum opens daily from 10.30 until 8pm in July and August, but it has shorter hours and closes on Mondays for the rest of the year.

Scan this QR code for opening hours and to book tickets.

★ TOP EXPERIENCE

San Juan de Gaztelugatxe

One of the most photographed features of the Basque coast is San Juan de Gaztelugatxe, a rocky island topped by a 10th-century hermitage, 10km northwest of Bermeo. The island is accessed from the mainland via a stone footbridge and steps.

MAP P86 **B2**

Approaching the Island

There are two entrance points for the descent to the **island** (bizkaia.eus/gaztelugatxe). The most popular route is the steep 1.2km walk from Eneperi, or from the upper car park, you can follow the path east to the Ermu starting point for a gentler but longer (1.6km) path down. You could descend one way and return the other. Allow about two hours in total. The site gets busy in summer, so early mornings are best.

Game of Thrones fans will recognise the setting, which was featured as Dragonstone in Season 7.

PLANNING TIP
Admission is free, but in summer and on autumn and spring weekends, you must book online in advance. Arrive promptly or you'll lose your slot. Wear trainers or hiking boots.

Scan this QR code for opening hours and to book tickets.

The Hermitage

From either approach, you access the island by crossing a stone bridge and climbing 241 steps. At the top is the small stone hermitage named after St John the Baptist, who, according to legend, once visited the island. Inside, the hermitage is adorned with nautical paraphernalia, including wooden oars and hanging model boats. The bow of a boat emerges from the wall above the altar. Look for the bell over the hermitage door. Legend has it that by ringing the bell three times, you will be granted a wish.

The island is a site of pilgrimages on 24 June, 31 July and 29 August.

JORGE SANCHEZ PHOTOS/SHUTTERSTOCK ©

ıatxitxako

rom the upper car park, a waymarked 4km hiking :ail leads along the coast to Cabo Matxitxako, a ape with two lighthouses. Allow about two hours ɔr the walk there and back; the lighthouses can lso be accessed by road. The older lighthouse ates from 1852 and was operated by a lighthouse eeper; the second was automatic and built in ɔ09. From the cape, there are fabulous views of an Juan de Gaztelugatxe.

In summer and autumn, look out for dolphins ıd whales, including common sperm whales, fin hales, pilot whales and even orcas. Matxitxako is so a good place to spot migratory birds, and the ɔlitary rock thrush and stonechat breed on the ıpe. You might also see peregrine falcons.

QUICK BREAK

You can't get much better views of San Juan de Gaztelugatxe than those from **Bar Gaztelu-Begi**. Pick up a *pintxo* (Basque tapa) and a coffee or beer.

WALKING TOUR

Walk the Central Basque Coast

The most spectacular way to approach Zumaia is via the coastal hiking trail from Deba, with outstanding views of the **flysch rock formations** (p92) along the way. This waymarked hiking trail climbs and descends over undulating cliffs where cows and sheep graze. Wear hiking boots and sun protection, and bring plenty of water and snacks.

START	END	LENGTH
Iglesia de Santa María, Deba	Zumaia	14km; four hours

1 Gothic Church

ɜegin in Deba's Plaza Zaharra, vhere the **Iglesia de Santa María** s a stop for pilgrims walking the ıorthern route of the Camino de ;antiago. Don't miss the magnifi-ent doorway decorated with the 2 apostles, angels and virgins.

2 Clifftop Hermitage

o begin the hike to Zumaia, look or the Talaia GR121 trail at the outhern side of the sports centre n Calle Mogel. From here, the oute is clearly signed with painted ed and white markings. A steady limb through grassy farmland rings you to the **Ermita de Santa ;atalina**, a small hermitage with weeping coastal views.

3 Fault Lines

'ext, look out for the white rock ıce of the **Aitzuri cliff wall**. hese cliffs were shaped by the ndutz fault line, which runs from orth to south and separates the :ack flysch (to the west) from the ıore recently formed calcareous ysch (to the east).

4 Surveying the Scene

n uphill climb brings you to the ›ectacular coastal lookout of **Iendatagaina**, where you can take a short (about 100m) signposted detour to a hilltop viewpoint.

5 Wave-Cut Rocks

At low tide, look for spiky, spine-like wave-cut platforms at **Playa de Sakoneta**. Sometimes covered by the ocean, these unusual formations were caused by seawater erosion. The cliff strata once lay horizontal but were shifted into a vertical position by the Earth's internal movements.

6 Dip in the Sea

Towards the end of the walk, some of the best views of the flysch can be seen on the final approach to Zumaia, by the Ermita de San Telmo. Allow time at **Playa Itzurun** to rest on the sand and dip your feet in the sea.

7 Return Journey

Under certain tidal conditions, **Flysch Boat Tours** (geoparkea.eus) offers boat trips between Zumaia and Deba (adult/child €16/€12); available dates are listed online. This makes it possible to see the flysch from land and sea, by walking one way and getting the boat the other. If the boat trip is not operating, Deba can be reached by train.

EXPERIENCES

Surf the Waves or Watch the Action in Mundaka

SURFING

MAP: 1 P86 C2

Mundaka is a big name in the surf world on account of its famous left-hand barrel. The wave breaks on a tapering sandbar formed by the outflow of the Río Urdaibai and, on a good day, offers heavy, barrelling lefts that can reel off for hundreds of metres.

Rent gear or book a lesson with **Mundaka Surf Shop** (mundaka surfshop.com; two-hour class €35). The shop also offers stand-up paddleboard equipment rentals and classes. One option is to paddle across the estuary to **Playa de Laida** (p93) and back.

Ride in a Boat Along the Flysch Coast

BOAT TRIP

MAP: 2 P86 F3

To view the flysch coast from the water, take an entertaining guided boat trip with **Flysch Boat Tours** (geoparkea.eus). The one-hour Essential Flysch Tour (adult/child €19/11) departs from Zumaia and travels along the coast towards Deba and back, with commentary along the way. Audio guides are available in English, French or German. Book ahead.

Spot Migratory Birds at Urdaibai Bird Center

BIRDWATCHIN

MAP: 3 P86 C3

The wetlands of the Urdaibai estuary are important resting sites for migratory birds, including spoonbills and osprey. You can learn all about them at the **Urdaibai Bird Center** (birdcenter.org; adult/chil €7/4). The centre is open daily in July and August, and at weekends only from September to June.

Exhibits include recordings of seasonal birdsong and live camera showing the wintering (South Africa) and summering (Norway and Iceland) locations of birds wh visit the area. At the observation deck, staff can help you spot and identify different species using binoculars and telescopes. The be times to see up to 200 species of migratory birds are May to June and September to October. Walking trails lead to two hides.

FLYSCH COAST

The 13km-long area between Mutriku and Zumaia forms the UNESCO **Basque Coast Geopark** on account of the unusual geological formations found there. Flysch are layers of sedimentary rock that jut out in distinct layers, revealing millions of years of the Earth's history. The flysch here are especially importan because of the extensive time between the earliest formations (roughly 110 millic years old) and the most recent (formed around 50 million years ago). What's more, the formations are in chronological order, allowing geologists to read the cliffs like a library of history books.

Take a Low-Tide Walk to Isla de San Nicolás

ISLAND

MAP: 4 P86 **D2**

Lekeitio is a lively, typically Basque seaside town that makes a great overnight stop. Its main attraction is **Isla de San Nicolás** (Garraitz Island), the rocky island sitting just offshore from the main beach (**Playa Isuntza**).

When tides are low, a paved path appears, allowing visitors to stroll out to the island and take the 200m trail to the top for fine views. Be mindful of the tides so that you don't have to swim back. The **tourist office** (MAP: 5 P86 D3) posts tidal charts. Allow about one hour in total.

Discover Txakoli Wine

VINEYARD

MAP: 8 P86 **B2**

If you like crisp, acidic, dry white wine, be sure to try *txakoli*. Using Hondarrabi Zuri grapes, *txakoli* is a fresh, slightly sparkling wine that goes well with seafood or *pintxos*. You can order *txakoli* by the glass in any Basque Country bar.

On the outskirts of Bakio, **Doniene Gorrondona** (doniene gorrondona.com) offers tours and tastings in English (€17 per person for a one-hour tour and tasting; book ahead).

Taste Wines Aged Underwater

WINERY

MAP: 9 P86 **A2**

Treat yourself to an underwater winery experience. In Plentzia, less than an hour by metro from Bilbao, **Crusoe Treasure** (underwaterwine.com) is a winery that ages its wines 20m below the surface of the ocean on an artificial reef.

Tastings are available on board during a two-hour scenic boat ride out to the reef, where bottles are hauled up from below. Cruises are offered from May to September (€94 per person; book ahead).

BEST BEACHES

Playa de Laida

MAP: 6 P86 **C2**

Where the water meets the shore, it's fairly shallow, making the golden sands of Laida great for families. Further out, you'll find good breaks for surfing. It's possible to paddle here by kayak or SUP from Mundaka.

Playa Itzurun

see 2 P86 **F3**

This dark sandy beach in Zumaia is wedged between the remarkable cliffs of the flysch coast. Its churning waters are notably clean.

Playa Isuntza

see 4 P86 **C3**

Lekeitio's sandy beach has views of Isla de San Nicolás.

Playa Zarautz

MAP: 7 P86 **F3**

This 2.5km-long beach is the Basque Country's longest and is a popular surfing spot.

LISTINGS

Best Places for...

See p86 for map of locations

€ Budget €€ Midrange €€€ Top End

Eating

Bermeo & Mundaka

Kai Alde €€
10 B2
This low-key restaurant at Bermeo's port serves freshly caught turbot, monkfish, cod and squid. *noon-11pm Tue-Sat, to 4pm Sun*

Restaurante Asador Portuondo €€€
11 C2
Overlooking the estuary, Portuondo serves char-grilled seafood alongside succulent steaks. *1.30-3.30pm Sun-Thu, 1.30-3.30pm & 9.15-10.15pm Fri & Sat; restaurante portuondo.com*

Luruna €€€
see 1 C2
Inside Mundaka's grand Palacio Larrinaga, this restaurant turns local seafood into seriously high-end plates. *1.30-3.30pm Wed-Sun, plus 8.30-10pm Jul & Aug; luruna.com*

Lekeitio

Mesón Arropain €€€
see 5 D3
This restaurant serves some of the best seafood around, including excellent *arrain zopa* (fish soup). *1.30-4.30pm & 8-10pm Fri & Sat, 1.30-4.30pm Sun*

Lumentza €
see 5 D3
This place is a local favourite. *Pintxos* include pickled anchovies with smoked salmon and quail egg, and Idiazabal cheese. *11am-3.30pm & 7pm-midnight Wed-Sun*

Kaia €
see 4 D2
Local tavern offering an array of *pintxos*, including excellent tortilla (Spanish omelette). *8am-11pm Sun-Thu, to 1am Fri & Sat*

Getaria

Elkano €€€
12 F3
One of the world's most famous seafood restaurants, where fish is grilled on a traditional wood fire. *1-3.15pm Tue-Thu, 1-3.15pm & 8.30-10pm Fri & Sat; restauranteelkano.com*

Kaia Kaipe €€€
see 12 F3
Enjoy harbour views and the smell of the grill as hake, sea bream and turbot cook on outdoor barbecues. *1-3.30pm Wed-Mon, plus 8-10.30pm Fri & Sat; kaia-kaipe.com*

Txoko Getaria €€€
see 12 F3
This breezy spot by the port is popular for its fresh sardines, sea bream and flounder fired up on the grill. *1-4pm Sun & Tue-Thu, to 11pm Fri & Sat; txokogetaria.com*

Zumaia, Mutriku & Zarautz

Idoia €€
see 2 F3
This Zumaia restaurant serves *pintxos* and small plates of contemporary seafood dishes like tuna tacos. *11.30am-5pm Mon, to 11.30pm Tue-Thu & Sun, 11.30am-12.30am Fri, to 1am Sat*

Taberna Ametza €€
13 E3
Ametza is an unfussy tavern that serves up some of the best cooking around. *11am-10.30pm*

Mon-Thu, to midnight Fri, 9am-1am Sat, to 6pm Sun

Pastelería Aizpurua €

see 14 F3

Artisan bakery and pastry shop in Zarautz's old town. Stop by for filled bagels, pastries and freshly baked pies. *8.30am-1pm & 4.30-7.30pm Tue-Sat, to 2pm Sun*

Okamika €€

see 14 F3

This chic Zarautz bar is the place to go for seafood *pintxos* and a glass of wine. *12.30-4pm & 7pm-midnight Sun-Tue, 7pm-midnight Thu, 12.30-4pm & 7pm-1am Fri & Sat; okamika.es*

Drinking

Ocean Views

Malako Kantina

see 10 B2

Offers craft beers from the Basque Country and beyond. It's perched on a hilltop overlooking a rocky beach just above Bermeo's old town. *10am-11pm*

Bar del Faro

see 5 D2

The terrace at this bar at the Santa Catalina lighthouse is perfect for a sunset drink with snacks. *11am-3pm & 5-8pm*

Txopos

see 1 C2

With one of the best terraces in Mundaka, Txopos is the go-to spot on clear days, with pretty views over the waterfront. *8am-1am Sun-Thu, to 2.30am Fri & Sat*

El Puerto

see 1 C2

With views of Mundaka harbour, the shady terrace at Hotel El Puerto is an appealing place to stop for a coffee or a glass of wine. *8am-midnight; hotelelpuerto.com*

Cocktails

Sukha

see 5 D3

Sophisticated, candlelit cocktail and wine bar serving select local cheeses, ham and *gildas* (anchovies with olives). *noon-11pm*

Shopping

Fashion & Accessories

Mundaka Basque Country

see 1 C2

Mundaka BC captures the town's free-spirited essence with its stylish clothing and accessories. The shop also has photography books and surf gear. *10am-2pm & 5-9pm Mon-Sat; mundakabc.com*

Flysch Aitzi

see 2 F3

This Zumaia boutique sells chic clothing and beachwear for women and children. *10am-1.30pm & 5-8pm Mon-Sat; flyschaitzi.com*

Cetaria

see 12 F3

Nautical striped clothing and Basque crafts are among the items for sale in this Getaria shop. *10.30am-8pm Mon & Wed-Sat*

Food & Drink

Merkatu Plaza

see 14 F3

Zarautz's market is the place to shop for seasonal local goodies, including fruits, vegetables, bread, cheeses and seafood. *8.30am-1.30pm & 5-8pm Mon-Fri, 8.30am-1.30pm Sat*

Amona María

see 12 F3

Portside delicatessen and *pintxo* bar in Getaria, selling local wines, cheeses, ham and sardines to eat in or take away. *11am-10pm Tue-Sun; amonamaria.com*

Explore San Sebastián

Worth a Trip

San Sebastián's Walking Tours

Street view and facade of Basílica de Santa María del Coro (p107)

FOTOKON/SHUTTERSTOCK ©

See p112
for eating, drinking and shopping listings

Explore Donostia-San Sebastián Parte Vieja

Officially named in both Basque (Donostia) and Spanish (San Sebastián), Donostia-San Sebastián is a city that celebrates the art of eating. Whether snacking on *pintxos* (Basque tapas) or lingering over a multicourse feast, experiencing the city's culinary scene is a decadent delight. The Parte Vieja (Old Quarter) is where you'll find San Sebastián's most famous *pintxo* bars, which line the neighbourhood's narrow pedestrianised streets. The neighbourhood is also home to the city's best museum, San Telmo Museoa. Behind it looms Monte Urgull, where tree-shaded trails lead to an old castle. Nearby, the old fishing port is overlooked by a fascinating aquarium.

Getting Around

Walking

Except for Paseo Nuevo (Pasealeku Berria), compact Parte Vieja is a pedestrianised zone, meaning walking is the best way to get around.

Bicycle

Loop around Monte Urgull using the ocean-side cycle lane on Paseo Nuevo. It's 2km from Puente de la Zurriola to the port.

Kayak

A fun way to reach Isla de Santa Clara is to hire a kayak or stand-up paddleboard from Darwin Rentals, which also rents scooters and bikes.

Donostia-San Sebastián
MEGAPIXELES.ES/SHUTTERSTOCK ©

★

THE BEST

SCULPTURE Construcción Vacía (p111)

PINTXOS Ganbara (p110)

MARINE LIFE Aquarium (p104)

VIEWPOINT Monte Urgull (p108)

MUSEUM San Telmo Museoa (p101)

Mar Cantábrico
(Kantauri Itsasoa)
For more see
Top Experiences p101
Experiences p108
Eating p112
Drinking p114
Shopping p115
Paseo Nuevo
Casa de la Historia
Castillo de la Mota
Monte Urgull
Construcción Vacía
San Telmo Museoa
Plaza de Zuloaga
Iglesia de San Vicente
Basílica de Santa María del Coro
Plaza de la Trinidad
La Viña
Plaza de la Constitución
Darwin Rentals
Ganbara
Paco Bueno
Plaza Carlos Blasco de Imaz
Aquarium
Euskal Itsas Museoa
Paseo del Muelle
Fishing Port
Bahía de la Concha
Motoras
Txepetxa
Enlargement
C de Narrica
C de la Pescadería
Bar Goiz-Argi
Bar Borda Berri
C de Fermín Calbetón
0
50 m
Paseo de Salamanca
Río Urumea
C de Aldamar
C de San Vicente
C de Iñigo
C de la Pescadería
C Euskal Herria
Puente de Kursaal
C 31 de Agosto
C Virgen de Coro
C del Puerto
C Mayor
C San Jerónimo
C de Esterlines
C de Narrica
C de San Lorenzo
Plaza Sarriegi
C de San Juan
Plaza la Bretxa
See Enlargement
C Mari Ijentea
C del Campanario
C de Embeltrán
Alameda del Boulevard
Blvd Zumardia
Blvd Reina Regente
C de Okendo
0
200 m

★ TOP EXPERIENCE

San Telmo Museoa

)ne of the Basque Country's best museums, **San Telmo Museoa** (adult/child €10/free; santelmomuseoa.eus) houses a hought-provoking collection that explores Basque history and ulture in all its complexity. Exhibitions are spread between a estored 16th-century convent and a contemporary new wing, lesigned to blend into its backdrop of Monte Urgull.

AP P100 **D2**

useum Design

he 16th-century Dominican convent which rms the original wing of the museum is a fusion f Gothic and Renaissance styles. The striking ontemporary new wing is covered with perforat-d aluminium sheets. The cladding is designed allow vegetation to emerge through the holes what looks like grey stone so that the building erges with Monte Urgull behind it.

ert Canvases

he highlight of the museum's permanent collec-on is the Sert Canvases, displayed in the dramatic tting of the convent church. These large-scale orks by Catalan artist Josep M Sert depict scenes om Basque history and mythology, including anels on shipbuilding, witchcraft and the oak ee of Gernika. They were completed in 1931 and ter painstakingly restored after incurring damage ecause of damp in the church walls. Get a better ew of the works from the 1st-floor gallery.

istory Galleries

he museum's telling of Basque history begins in e **Traces of Spirituality** gallery, appropriately

PLANNING TIP
The museum is closed on Monday and free on Tuesday. Labelling is mostly in Spanish and Basque. Audio guides are available in other languages.

Scan this QR code for opening hours and to book tickets.

JJFARQ/SHUTTERSTOCK ©

QUICK BREAK
San Telmo Museoa's in-house restaurant **Zazpi STM** has two spaces, a *taberna* (tavern) serving drinks and high-end *pintxos*, and a more formal restaurant.

located in the cloister. Housed here is a collection of steles (Basque funeral stones, used to mark the place of burial or the place of death) and *argizaiolak* (wooden boards wrapped in thin wax candles placed on tombs in churches). The oldest steles date from Roman times. Look for astral symbology, geometric motifs and pagan elements, which continued to be used after the arrival of Christianity.

Next is the **Memory Traces** gallery, which looks at the origins of Basque culture and traditional daily life, and how the Basques began to interact with the outer world when they set off by boat to explore it. The gallery has good information on the more than 12,000-year-old paintings in the caves of Ekain, Altxerri and Santimamiñe. Items on display include whale-hunting spears. Don't miss the 18th-century telescope belonging to José Joaquín Ferrer, an expert in astronomy and cartography.

Famed fashion designer Cristóbal Balenciaga created the collection of Basque women's head-dresses, once a symbol of wealth and status. In the 17th century, headdresses like these were banned because of their scandalous phallic shape.

On the 1st floor, the largest exhibition space houses **Awakening Modernity**, which covers the transformations in Basque society that took place during the 19th and 20th centuries, when lifestyles changed from rural to industrial and urban. Exhibits range from traditional farming equipment to 1960s pop culture. Don't miss the traditional Basque musical instruments, including the *txalaparta* (an improvised wooden percussion instrument) and *alboka* horns.

Art Collection

Completing the Awakening Modernity exhibition is **100 Years of Basque Art**, displaying pieces from the avant-garde artists of the 1920s through to the present day. The works are grouped by theme, including industry and feminism.

Up a modern staircase, the 2nd-floor gallery houses the museum's **Fine Arts Historical Collection**, with pieces from the 15th through the 20th century. Look for works by El Greco, Rubens, Tintoretto and Fortuny, as well as Basque artists. One room is mostly dedicated to the large canvases of Antonio Ortiz Echagüe, whose paintings include scenes depicting Morocco in the 1930s.

Temporary Exhibitions

Check the website to see what temporary exhibitions are being staged. The museum is known for its thoughtfully curated shows, covering diverse themes from the history of human exile and migration to 1990s art.

THE SITE'S HISTORY

San Telmo was founded in the 16th century for an order of Dominican monks and survived the fire of 31 August 1813 (p108), which destroyed much of the city. After the monks were expelled in 1836, the building became a military barracks. In 1932, it was converted into a museum, and the extension was completed in 2011.

★ TOP EXPERIENCE

Aquarium

Brace yourself in the aquarium's tunnel as you stand surrounded by fish while sharks swim overhead. This maritime museum and **aquarium** (adult/child €14/7; aquariumss.com) tells the story of the underwater world beyond Donostia-San Sebastián's shores and how the people of the city interact with and depend on the sea.

MAP P100 **A4**

PLANNING TIP
Labelling is in Spanish, Basque and English. Allow at least 1½ hours to see everything, though you could spend several hours watching the tanks.

Scan this QR code for opening hours and ticket prices.

Maritime Exhibition

Begin on the 2nd floor in the marine history galleries, which explore the Basques' long and adventurous seafaring past. They were accomplished whalers and in-demand navigators. Displays cover early maritime trade and continues through boat-racing customs and the evolution of San Sebastián's port. The Gipuzkoa Oceanographic Society, founded in 1908, collected many of the items on display. Highlights include model ships and the 11m-long skeleton of a North Atlantic right whale.

Next, view marine-themed artworks, including *The Tuna*, a piece constructed with empty cans found at the beach. Don't miss the beautifully backlit display of seashells. A gallery space houses temporary exhibitions of sea-related works.

Bay of Biscay Aquariums

Some of the first tanks you'll see are of mesmerising jellyfish as you approach the aquarium's biggest draw: the 13m-by-13.5m oceanarium tank, which houses 40 species of fish from the neighbouring Cantabrian Sea and Atlantic Ocean. The seawater in the tank is pumped in from La Concha Bay.

The highlight is the glass tunnel. As you walk through, you'll see sand tiger sharks (aka dogfish

KATRINN/SHUTTERSTOCK ©

sharks), small sharks (smooth-hounds, small-spotted catsharks and nursehounds), turbots, guitarfish and other denizens of the deep approaching from all sides, including underfoot. Shark feedings take place at noon on Tuesdays, Thursdays and Saturdays.

A favourite with children is the tactile tank, where they can handle sea urchins and starfish. It's also possible to book an aquarium sleepover for your family – you'll spend the night tucked into a sleeping bag in the tunnel as sharks swim around you.

Tropical Aquariums

Next, take a look at oversized tanks of beautiful corals and bright tropical marine fish. The 18m-long mangrove swamp display reveals some of the unusual creatures that live in this unique environment. Don't miss the clownfish and seahorses.

QUICK BREAK
The aquarium doesn't have an on-site cafe, but the surrounding port has several seafood restaurants, including **Kofradia**.

WALKING TOUR

Walk Parte Vieja

It wouldn't take long to stroll from one end of the compact Parte Vieja to the other if there weren't so many distractions along the way. From innumerable *pintxo* bars to the market stalls that supply them, and intriguing public artworks, it's easy to lose track of time as you wander the streets.

START	END	LENGTH
Mercado de la Bretxa	Iglesia de San Vicente	0.8km; one hour

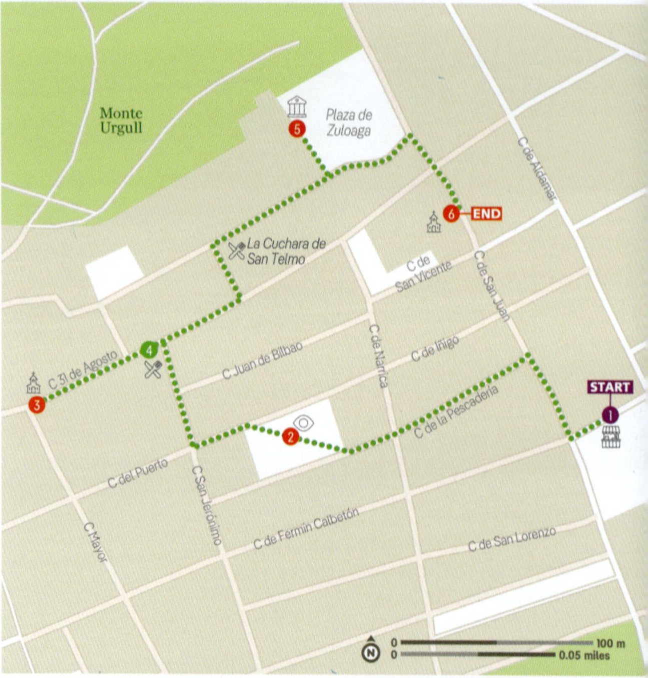

1 Produce Market

The Pescadaría (fish market) building of **Mercado de la Bretxa** dates from 1870. Today, traditional market stalls are located on the building's lower floor. In front of the building, look for more stalls selling local cheeses, fresh flowers, and fresh fruit and vegetables.

2 Pretty Square

At the heart of the Parte Vieja is **Plaza de la Constitución**, one of the Basque Country's most stunning squares, It was built in 1817 on the site of an older square, following the devastating fire of 1813 (p108). The square was once used as a bullring, and the balconies of the fringing houses were rented to spectators.

3 Baroque Basilica

Walk one block west and then turn right onto Calle Mayor then left onto Calle 31 de Agosto. Before you is the Parte Vieja's most photogenic building, the baroque **Basílica de Santa María del Coro**, completed in 1774. Its ornate facade depicts St Sebastián. Inside is an altarpiece dedicated to San Sebastián's other patron saint, Our Lady of the Choir.

4 *Pintxo* Bars

Calle 31 de Agosto is lined with some of the city's best *pintxo* bars, including **Gandarias**. Turn left up Calle de Valle Lersundi Plaza to reach **La Cuchara de San Telmo**, where you can stop for a *pintxo*. Afterwards, continue east along Santa Korda to reach Plaza de Zuloaga.

5 Architecture Old & New

In Plaza de Zuloaga, look at the old and new wings of **San Telmo Museoa**. Looming behind is the forested Monte Urgull. You might see children playing ball games in the square.

6 Historic Church

The striking **Iglesia de San Vicente** is the oldest building in San Sebastián. Its origins date to the late 12th century, but it was rebuilt in its current Gothic form in the early 1500s. Behind its towering facade lies a vaulted interior, featuring an elaborate gold altarpiece and a 19th-century French organ. Don't miss the stained-glass windows.

EXPERIENCES

Admire the Views from Monte Urgull

VIEWPOINT

MAP: 1 P100 B3

For breathtaking views, walk to the summit of **Monte Urgull** (123m) along one of several routes: by taking a path from behind the new wing of the San Telmo Museoa in Plaza de Zuloaga, via the steps behind Basílica de Santa María del Coro or on the path from the Aquarium. The shady woodland on the way up is a peaceful retreat from the city. Allow about an hour for the walk to the top and back.

Beneath the trees, near the English cemetery, look for Eduardo Chillida's *Torso homenaje a Pedro Arana* (Torso in Tribute to Pedro Arana), a bronze the artist made in homage to a friend.

At the summit stands a statue of Christ and the stone fortress of **Castillo de la Mota** (MAP: 2 P100 C2), the latest incarnation of many fortifications that have existed here since the 12th century.

Visit Monte Urgull's Castle Museum

MUSEUM

MAP: 3 P100 B2

Inside Castillo de la Mota is **Casa de la Historia**, a free small museum focusing on the city's history (open daily in July and August, and weekends only from April to June and September to October). For most people, half an hour is enough time to look around.

The museum has audiovisual exhibits that touch on Donostia-San Sebastián's traditional festivals and display historical artefacts (including military uniforms used in the Carlist Wars), as well as photographs and models showing the city's evolution over the years.

On the 1st floor, look for the spiral staircase leading to the rooftop, with spectacular views of Playa de la Concha and the city.

Take a Boat Trip to Isla de Santa Clara

ISLAND

MAP: 4 P100 A3

Lying 500m offshore, the little island of **Isla de Santa Clara** is

DISASTROUS FIRE

Calle 31 de Agosto, at the northern end of the Parte Vieja, commemorates one of the darker days in San Sebastián's history. On 31 August 1813, an army of allied troops from England and Portugal captured the city from France during the Napoleonic Wars, ransacked it and then burnt it down. Only a handful of houses and the churches of **San Vicente** and the **Basílica de Santa María del Coro** survived. Today, candles are lit on the balconies lining this street every 31 August.

HOW TO EAT *PINTXOS*

The people of Donostia-San Sebastián enjoy nothing more than strolling from bar to bar with friends, sampling one *pintxo* after another. Inside the bars, the counters are piled high with small plates of *pintxos*, such as prawn or salmon mouse on a sliver of bread, skewers of squid or octopus, quail eggs, mushrooms, and foie gras. Most bars also offer made-to-order hot *pintxos*, which are listed on a board behind the bar. Order your *pintxos* from the bartender and eat them wherever there's space (often standing up).

accessible by a 10-minute boat trip with **Motoras de la Isla** (motoras delaisla.com; MAP: 5 P100 **D4**). Boats run every half hour from the Parte Vieja fishing port from June to September (return trip €4).

You can also paddle to Santa Clara by stand-up paddleboard or kayak. Rent one from **Darwin Rentals** (darwinrentals.es; €12 per hour; MAP: 6 P100 **C3**) in Parte Vieja.

At low tide, the island gains its own tiny beach. There are also picnic tables and a summertime kiosk. Climb the forested path to the small lighthouse housing an art installation.

Allow two or three hours for the trip to the island and back, with time to explore, eat a picnic and swim in the sea.

Watch Waves Wash Over a Seabed Sculpture

PUBLIC ART

MAP: 7 P100 **A4**

A five-minute walk from the ferry pier on Isla de Santa Clara, a small lighthouse now houses **Hondalea** (artingenium.com/casa-del-faro), an installation by local artist Cristina Iglesias. Inside the hollowed-out 19th-century lighthouse building, Iglesias has created a bronze sculpture of the seabed (*hondalea* is a Basque word meaning both abyss and bottom of the sea). Water is pumped over the sculpture to create the effect of a churning ocean.

The installation is free of charge and can be accessed in small groups. Viewings are every 30 minutes. After the guide's introduction, you can walk around the viewing platforms, watching the waves lapping over the sculpture, for up to 20 minutes.

Discover San Sebastián's Maritime History at Euskal Itsas Museoa

MUSEUM

MAP: 8 P100 **B4**

Overlooking the Parte Vieja's fishing port, the free-to-visit **Euskal Itsas Museoa** (itsasmuseoa.eus) has exhibitions exploring the Basques' relationship with the sea. It's closed on Monday. The galleries occupy two floors of a mid-18th-century building (one of the few to survive the 1813 fire), which was once used by the San Sebastián Merchants' Guild.

The museum hosts long-term temporary exhibitions, which in the past have featured thoughtful takes on themes such as shipwrecks, women and the sea, and slavery. It also has displays of marine-themed art and photography. Signage is in English, Spanish, Basque and French.

Feast on *Pintxos* PINTXOS

MAP: 9 P100 D3

Grazing on *pintxos* is the best way to sample San Sebastián's famously good food. The city's best-known *pintxo* bars are in Parte Vieja, along Calle 31 de Agosto and near **Plaza de la Constitución**.

Many bars are known for their house specialities. Start with the *gambas a la gabardina* (battered prawns), made fresh to order at **Paco Bueno** (MAP: 13 P100 D4 ; closed Thursday evening and all day Friday). The grilled mushrooms with poached egg *pintxo* is the house speciality at **Ganbara** (MAP: 14 P100 D3; ganbarajatetxea.com; closed Sunday and Monday). Next, try the anchovies at **Txepetxa** (MAP: 15 P100 E1; bartxepetxa.es; closed Monday), another traditional San Sebastián *pintxo* bar. At old-school **Bar Borda Berri** (MAP: 16 P100 E1; closed Sunday and Monday), order the sheep's cheese risotto. On the same street is **Bar Goiz-Argi** (MAP: 17 P100 F1), where brochetas de gambas (prawn skewers) are the house speciality.

Taste La Viña's Famous Basque Cheesecake FOOD

MAP: 18 P100 E3

Though you'll want to sample as many of the Parte Vieje's delicious *pintxos* as possible, be sure to leave room for dessert. The bar and restaurant **La Viña** (lavina restaurante.com; closed Monday) is famous for its baked cheesecake, prepared daily and left to cool on shelves by the bar. Since opening La Viña in 1959, the Rivera family has used the same recipe to make their creamy baked cheesecake with a perfectly burnt crust, a tradition continued by their son Santiago Rivera today. Order a slice (€6) to eat at the bar.

TXOTX TO CIDER

With a climate suited to growing apples, the province of Gipuzkoa is known for its cider (*sagardoa* in Basque, *sidra* in Spanish). Basque cider has a tart taste, and to add a little fizz, it must be poured into the glass from a height. You can try it in San Sebastián's bars. Outside the city, you can visit a *sagardotegi*, a rural cider house that also serves food. Traditionally, someone periodically calls out '*txotx*' (pronounced 'chotch'). This is the cue to head to the cider barrels, where the tap is opened and everyone fills up.

See Sculptures by Jorge Oteiza

PUBLIC ART

MAP: 10 P100 **A3**

One of the joys of exploring Donostia-San Sebastián is discovering sculptures by Basque artists.

At the base of Monte Urgull is Jorge Oteiza's **Construcción Vacía** (Empty Space) sculpture. Oteiza (1908–2003) was a renowned painter, sculptor and writer who was born and brought up close to Donostia-San Sebastián. An award winner at the 1957 São Paulo Biennale, this rust-red work looks out towards the sea. For a different angle, climb part way up Monte Urgull to view it from above. It's a particularly beautiful spot at sunset.

Another piece by Oteiza can be seen at **Iglesia de San Vicente** (MAP: 11 P100 E3). Piedad depicts a seated Virgin Mary with her arms raised, and Christ lying across her lap. Orteiza himself chose the location for the piece. Look for it on the exterior wall near the side entrance to the church on Calle San Vicente.

Discover Religious & Contemporary Art in a Baroque Basilica

BASILICA

MAP: 12 P100 **D3**

With an eye-catching decorative portico, the baroque **Basílica de Santa María del Coro** (adult/child €3/free; dmuseoa.com) houses a religious art collection with pieces from the Middle Ages to the 20th century.

Mounted on the basilica's back wall and beautifully lit is *Gurutz III* (Alabaster Cross) by Eduardo Chillida. Created in 1975, the piece is one of a series of similar works. The shape of the cross is created with negative space.

On the basilica's exterior wall near the portico, look for the sculpture *The Harmony of Sound* by Maximilian Pelzmann. The wave-like shapes and spaces reference musical notes.

FESTIVALS

Throughout the year, the Parte Vieja is a scene of celebration during Donostia-San Sebastián's major festivals.

Día de San Sebastián
Revellers fill Plaza de la Constitución to see the drumming bands of the Tamborrada in January.

Aste Nagusia (Semana Grande)
Street parties, concerts and parades are held across the city during this August festival.

Feria de Santo Tomás
In December, Plaza de Zuloaga is one of several locations used to stage events, involving livestock exhibitions, traditional games and stalls selling countryside produce.

LISTINGS

Best Places for...

€ Budget €€ Midrange €€€ Top End

See p100 for map of locations

Eating

Traditional Pintxo Bars

Bar Martínez €
19 D3
Opening its doors in the 1940s, tiny Bar Martínez' *pintxos* include courgette parcels filled with creamy spider crab. *noon-6pm & 7-11pm Sat-Wed, 7-11pm Fri; barmartinezdonosti.com*

Casa Vergara €
20 D3
Bustling *pintxos* spot where the bar is piled high with food, including some tasty vegetarian options. *11am-10.30pm Sun-Thu, to 11pm Fri & Sat; grupogarrancho.com*

Bar Sport €
21 E1
People flock to this *pintxos* place for its Basque bites, such as *txangurro* crepe (spider crab pancake). *9am-midnight Mon-Fri, from 10am Sat, 11am-midnight Sun*

Tamboril €
22 E1
This *pintxo* bar has outdoor seating in a prime location on Plaza de la Constitución. Try the mushrooms. *12.30-3.30pm & 7-11pm Tue-Sat*

Gourmet Pintxos

La Cuchara de San Telmo €
23 D3
Creative chefs offer made-to-order *pintxos*, and the menu is written on a chalkboard behind the bar. *noon-4pm & 7-11pm Tue-Sun*

Gandarias €
24 D3
This bar offers an extensive selection of artfully presented *pintxos*. Try the crab pie. Its restaurant serves classic Basque dishes. *11am-midnight; restaurantegandarias.com*

Txalupa Gastroleku €
25 F1
The bar is shaped like a *txalupa* (traditional fishing boat) and piled high with sublime *pintxos*. *10am-midnight Sun-Thu, to 12.30am Fri & Sat*

Beti-Jai Berria €
26 E3
This contemporary *pintxo* bar offers views of the kitchen so you can watch the chefs at work. *noon-11.30pm Thu-Tue, plus Wed Jul & Aug; betijaiberria.eus*

Basque

Bar Nestor €€
27 E3
This place is known for its juicy steaks. The tortilla is also legendary but usually sells out early. *1-3.30pm & 8-10.30pm Tue-Sat; 1-3.30pm Sun*

Restaurante Muxumartín €€€
28 D4
A fresh, creative approach to typical Basque dishes. Book a table for a sit-down meal or snack on *pintxos* in the bar. *12.30-3.30pm & 7-10.30pm; muxumartin.com*

Casa Urola €€€
29 E3
The restaurant at Casa Urola offers a traditional Basque menu, including plenty of seafood. The bar serves excellent *pintxos*.

noon-3.15pm & 7-11.15pm Thu-Mon; casaurolajate txea.es

Txuleta ❸❸❸

30 D3

Txuleta is a cut of beef, and this is the place to taste melt-in-your-mouth steaks. The bar serves bite-size samples. *noon-4pm & 7-11pm Wed-Sun, noon-4pm Mon; txuleta restaurante.com*

Splash-Out Meals

Kokotxa ❸❸❸

31 C3

This Michelin-starred restaurant offers two different meal-of-a-lifetime tasting menus, served to the whole table. Book well in advance. *1.30-2.30pm & 8.30-9.30pm Tue-Sat; restaura ntekokotxa.com*

Astelena ❸❸❸

32 F3

Classic Basque cooking with modern touches, served in a former banana store turned smart dining room. *1.30-3pm & 8.30-10pm; restaurante astelena.com*

Zazpi STM ❸❸❸

33 E2

The chic restaurant at the San Telmo museum serves beautifully presented plates of contemporary Basque cuisine. *1-3pm Tue & Wed, 1-3pm & 8-10pm Thu, to 11pm Fri & Sat; zazpistm.com*

Bodegón Alejandro ❸❸❸

34 F1

This cellar restaurant is acclaimed for its traditional Basque cooking of seasonal local ingredients, such as cod, hake, steak and mushrooms. *1-3pm & 8-10pm; bodegonalejandro.com*

Seafood

Restaurante Marinela ❸❸❸

35 B3

Overlooking the fishing port, Marinela serves sharing plates and individual servings of freshly caught seafood. *noon-4pm & 7.30-11pm Mon-Sat, noon-4pm Sun; marineladonostia.com*

Kaskazuri ❸❸❸

36 E2

Serves upmarket Basque seafood. The weekday lunchtime *menu del día* is a good deal (three courses for €27.50). *1-3.30pm & 8.30-11pm; kaskazuri.com*

La Mejíllonera ❸❸

37 D4

Come to La Mejíllonera for mussels prepared in a variety of ways. All go down nicely with *patatas bravas* (fried potatoes in a spicy sauce) and a cold beer. *11.30am-3pm & 6-11.45pm; cerveceriasla mejillonera.es*

Kofradia ❸❸❸

38 C3

At the port, this contemporary, laid-back restaurant specialises in seasonal fish sustainably sourced from local boats. *10.30am-5.45pm Wed, to 10pm Thu-Sat, to 3.30pm Sun; kofradia.eus*

Italian

Raviolina ❸❸

39 D3

This buzzing Italian restaurant serves thin-crust pizzas and an array of antipasti and pasta. *12.30pm-11pm Sun-Mon & Wed-Thu, to 11.30pm Fri & Sat; raviolina restaurante.com*

Ice Cream & Cake

Gelatería Boulevard ❸

40 E4

For something sweet, order a scoop of Italian-style gelato from Gelatería Boulevard. There's another branch at the Kursaal. *11am-1.30am Sun-Thu, to 2am Fri & Sat; gelateriaboulevard.es*

Carlos Arribas ❸

41 D3

This place has earned a local following for its decadent ice cream. Flavours include pistachio, raspberry, hazelnut, coconut, and cheesecake with berries. *12.30pm-11.30pm; carlosarribas.eu*

Bassk Cheesecakers ⓢ
42 F3
Buy traditional San Sebastián baked cheesecake by the slice or the pie from this specialist bakery. Cakes are displayed in the window to woo passersby. *10am-2pm & 5-8pm; basskcheesecakers.com*

Drinking

Coffee

Motx
43 D4
This small specialty coffee shop serves drinks made with Sakona beans (roasted in Irun) as well as pastries. *8am-6pm*

Syra Coffee
44 E4
One of four San Sebastián branches of the Barcelona coffee shop, offering an array of beans and pours, including cold brews. *8am-8pm; syra.coffee*

Colors Coffee by Sakona
45 E4
Inside Loco Market clothes store, this tiny coffee shop serves pours made with Sakona beans, alongside baked goods. *8.30am-6pm*

Cocktails

Côte Bar
46 D4
Stylish bar where you can sip on well-made cocktails. Live music some nights. *10pm-3am Wed & Thu, 7pm-4am Fri & Sat, 10pm-3am Sun*

Sybaris Coctelería
47 D4
At this high-end cocktail bar, you can tell the bartenders what you want and they'll create it. *6.30pm-1am Mon-Thu, 5.30pm-2am Fri & Sat, to 1am Sun; sybaris cocteleria.com*

Pubs

Garua Bar
48 E3
This bar has Basque craft beer on tap and serves a menu of burgers and nachos. *6.30-11.30pm Wed-Fri, 1.30-5pm & 7pm-1am Sat, 1.30-5pm & 7-11.30pm Sun*

Hole Pub
49 E3
Old-school rock music and darts are the defining features of this underground bar. *6pm-3am Sun-Thu, to 4am Fri & Sat*

Music & Dancing

Arkaitzpe
50 D3
DJs play most nights (nightly in summer) in this bar's basement. The cocktails pack a punch. *9pm-3am Sun-Thu, 6pm-4.30am Fri & Sat*

Be Club
51 F3
As well as offering a long list of cocktails, this little club has DJs and dancing until late. *3pm-5am Sun-Thu, to 6.30am Fri & Sat; beclubss.com*

Drinks With a View

Urgulleko Polboriña
52 A3
Partway up Monte Urgull, this terrace is the perfect place for a glass of wine or a beer, with unbeatable views of Isla de Santa Clara. *11am-8.45pm*

LGBTIQ+

Dioni's
53 D4
This glam cocktail bar hosts an LGBTIQ+ disco

on Friday and Saturday nights. *8.30am-9pm Sun-Thu, to 4.30am Fri & Sat; dionispub.com*

Shopping

Food & Drink

Aitor Lasa

54 F3

This high-quality deli sells an array of cheeses, mushrooms, and seasonal fruit and vegetables. *10.30am-2pm & 5-8pm Mon-Fri, 8.30am-2.30pm Sat; aitorlasa.com*

Goñi Ardoteka

55 E3

Run by three sisters since the 1970s, this little wine shop is stocked full of bottles. *10.30am-2pm & 4-7.30pm Mon-Fri, 10.30am-2pm Sat; ardoteka.com*

Mercado de la Bretxa

56 F3

Accessed via escalators in a glass kiosk-like building, this covered market is an ideal place to stock up on picnic supplies. *8am-8pm Mon-Sat; bretxa.eus*

Art & Music

Beltza Records

57 F1

Browse for vinyl and CDs from the Basque Country and beyond at this chequerboard-tiled record shop. *11am-1.30pm & 4-8pm Mon-Sat; beltzarecords.com*

Koloreka

58 D4

Art shop selling graphic prints of San Sebastián scenes, available with a custom frame and packaging to keep it safe in your suitcase. *noon-8pm Mon-Sat, to 5pm Sun; koloreka.com*

Crafts & Gifts

Alboka Artesanía

59 E3

Crafts and objects made in the Basque Country fill this shop on one of the old town's prettiest plazas. *10.30am-8pm Mon-Sat, 11am-3pm; albokaartesania.com*

Nómada

60 E2

For something really special, check out the exquisite rugs and carpets here, sourced from all over the world by the proprietors. *10.30am-7.30pm Mon-Sat; nomada.biz*

Room 278

61 C3

Sells prints of San Sebastián, printed canvas bags, mugs, t-shirts and more. *9.30am-1.30pm & 4.30-7.30pm Mon-Fri; room278shop.com*

Fashion & Accessories

La Soupe by Vintage Closet

62 E1

Browse this vintage clothing store for fun, retro styles as well as statement accessories. *noon-4pm & 5.30-9pm Tue-Fri, noon-4.30pm & 5-9pm Sat, noon-7pm Sun*

Casa Ponsol

63 E4

In business since 1838, this hat shop evokes a bygone era. It stocks a range of styles, including *boinas* (berets). *10am-1.30pm & 4-8pm Mon-Sat; casaponsol.com*

Pukas

64 D4

Branch of the legendary San Sebastián surf shop, selling surfboards, beachwear and surf-related paraphernalia. *10am-8.30pm Mon-Thu, from noon Fri, 10.30am-9pm Sat, noon-8pm Sun; pukassurfshop.com*

See p129
for eating, drinking and shopping listings

A
B
C
D
1
2
3
4
5
6
Mar Cantábrico (Kantauri Itsasoa)
Isla de Santa Clara
Bahía de la Concha (Kontxako Badia)
Funicular Railway (550m)
1
6 Playa de Ondarreta
Monte Igueldo
Pico del Loro
9 Abrazo
4
17
Av de Satrustegui
Av de Zumalkarregi
Plaza de Alfonso XIII
8 Palacio Miramar
10 Monumento a Fleming
Paseo de la Concha
Paseo de Miraconcha
38
25
7 Jardines de Miramar
ANTIGUO
C de Matia
C Erregezain
For more see
Top Experiences p120
Experiences p126
Eating p129
Drinking p130
Shopping p130
0 500 m
0 0.25 miles

E
F
G
H
1
2
3
4
5
6
PARTE VIEJA
Paseo del Muelle
Fishing Port
C Mari Ijentea
C Mayor
Alameda del Boulevard
Blvd Reina Regente
Puente de Kursaal
Río Urumea
Paseo de la República Argentina
Teatro Victoria Eugenia
Mimo Bite the Experience
C Bengoechea
C de Okendo
C Sta Catalina
C de Hernani
C Peñaflorida
C Elkano
C Andia
C de Garibai
Paseo de los Fueros
C Etxaide
C Bergara
Plaza de Cervantes
Av de la Libertad
C Getaria
C Hondarribia
C de Loyola
C de Urbieta
C de Arasate
C de San Martín
Plaza del Buen Pastor
C Valentín Olano
Paseo de la Concha
Club Deportivo Fortuna
C de Zubieta
C de Manterola
C del Triunfo
C de la Marina
C San Bartolomé
C de Urdaneta
C de los Reyes Católicos
C de Prim
Koldo Mitxelena Kulturunea
C de Larramendi
C de Easo
C de Moraza
Paseo de Árbol de Guernica
Playa de la Concha
La Perla
Cuesta de Aldapeta
Parque Basoerdi
Amara Train Station (ET/FV)
C de Egana

★ TOP EXPERIENCE

Playa de la Concha

A perfect city beach, Playa de la Concha is framed by the Parte Vieja (Old Quarter), beautiful parks and elegant belle époque buildings. Sunbathers spread across the sand throughout the summer months, when a party atmosphere prevails. Its sheltered position means swimming is almost always safe.

MAP P118 **E4**

PLANNING TIP
Lifeguards patrol the beach from 9am to 8.30pm in July and August, from 9am to 8pm in June and September, and from 10am to 6pm in April, May, and October.

Scan this QR code for Club Deportivo Fortuna's opening hours and prices.

Sand & Sea

In summer, Playa de la Concha is a hive of activity. Swim out to floating diving platforms and zip down the slides, or join in a volleyball match on the sand. At the eastern end of the beach, look for sand artists creating sculptures that are washed away with the tide.

Club Deportivo Fortuna (cdfortunake.com) rents out kayaks, stand-up paddleboards and surfboards from the beachside kiosk (one/two hours €13/20, open daily June to September, weekend mornings only October to May). Options include a paddle out to **Isla de Santa Clara** (p108).

At the eastern end of the beach are accessible hot showers, changing rooms and lockers (€2.50, plus a €6.50 cash deposit) and an accessible ramp down to the sand. From June to September, a free assisted bathing service is available to people with reduced mobility (it's located by the lifeguard station near the clocks).

The beach gets crowded in August, with a party vibe. If you prefer to have more space on the sand, come in the morning. The sea is still chilly as late as June, but you can use the hot showers to warm up after a swim in the cooler months. (You'll see hardy souls taking a dip year-round.)

CEDRIC_CLV/SHUTTERSTOCK ©

Seafront Promenade

Curving around the 1.3km-long beach is **Paseo de la Concha**, an elegant promenade. Lined by an ornamental wrought-iron balustrade, it's a wonderful place for a jog or stroll, particularly in the early evening when everyone comes out to enjoy the bracing sea air and soft summer light. You can also zip along the adjacent cycle path.

After dark, the promenade is illuminated by belle époque lampposts, with magical views of the city's lights reflecting in the lapping water.

Roughly halfway along the beach is the belle époque **La Perla** (p126) spa and restaurant complex, an ornate 1912 pavilion that was once the royal bathing house but is now open to all.

QUICK BREAK
Built into the pavilions that back the beach is the Art Deco **Cafe de la Concha**, which has all-day dining and out-of-this-world views.

★ TOP EXPERIENCE

Monte Igueldo

At the far western end of the Bahía de la Concha is the fun-filled **Monte Igueldo** (monteigueldo.es). Attractions include a historic funicular railway to the summit and a funfair at the top, with rides to get the adrenaline pumping. It's also the starting point for coastal hikes. The views are particularly beautiful at sunset.

MAP P118 **A4**

PLANNING TIP
The funicular, lookout enclosure and funfair rides have different opening hours. With the exception of the Christmas and Easter holidays, the funfair rides operate weekends only from late September to mid June.

Scan this QR code for opening hours and prices.

Funicular Railway

Clattering up and down Monte Igueldo since 1912, the **funicular railway** (return trip adult/child €4.50/2.50) transports passengers to the summit. Evoking San Sebastián's early 20th-century heyday, the original wooden carriages slide through the trees and emerge to breathtaking views of the bay. It departs every 15 minutes.

Funfair & Tower

At 181m high, Monte Igueldo is the highest point in the city. The striking **Torreón de Monte Igueldo** is a fortified former lighthouse dating from the mid-18th century, which replaced an earlier light signal from the 16th century. After a new lighthouse was built in 1854, the original tower was reconstructed in 1912 to serve as a lookout for visitors. It looks out over the vast panorama of the Bahía de la Concha and the surrounding coastline and mountains.

Also at the top of Monte Igueldo is an old-fashioned **amusement park**. The star attraction is the Swiss Mountain roller coaster, where you can catch glimpses of the incredible views as you whoosh by. Other rides include a log flume, a horror house, a boat pond, bumper cars and a carousel.

Admission to the lookout (the enclosed area around the tower and attractions) is included in

SAIKO3P/SHUTTERSTOCK ©

the funicular ticket price, but if you arrive on foot or by car, you must pay to enter the lookout zone (€2.50). Each funfair ride has an additional cost.

Canopy & Hikes

Another Monte Igueldo attraction is **Canopy**,(canopy donostiaventura.com) a high ropes and zip-line course through the pine trees. The 420m canopy circuit includes 14 zip lines, and there is also a shorter adventure circuit. Allow 1½ hours for both (adult/child €23/20). There is a minimum height requirement of 1.4m. It's best to book in advance.

For a scenic hike up Monte Igueldo, follow the **Camino de Santiago** trail from Playa de Ondarreta. For a longer hike, you could follow the trail through beautiful countryside as far as Orio (16km).

WALKING TOUR

Walk San Sebastián's New Town

A scenic area for strolling, San Sebastián's New Town, or Centro Romántico, has tree-shaded landscaped parks and wide, straight streets lined by stately belle époque buildings. With Playa de la Concha on one side and the Río Urumea on the other, you're never far from the water and wonderful views.

START	END	LENGTH
Ayuntamiento	Real Club Náutico de San Sebastián	2.5km; one hour

1 Domed City Hall

Start at San Sebastián's **Ayuntamiento** (City Hall), an impressive configuration of belle époque towers and domed ceilings. It began life as the Gran Casino in 1887 before becoming the city hall in 1947.

2 Pretty Plaza

In front of the city hall is **Parque de Alderdi Eder**. One of the liveliest little outdoor spaces in San Sebastián, the park is an elongated plaza shaded by trees and busy with children and families enjoying the old-fashioned carousel and street performers. Beautiful views unfold over Playa de la Concha.

3 Emblematic Square

Walk two blocks east along Calle Andia to reach **Plaza de Gipuzkoa**. Designed in 1877, the square has a duck pond and a stream crossed by a little footbridge. A pergola shelters a meteorological barometer, a planetary chart and a statue of pianist and composer José María Usandizaga.

4 Centre Stage

Continue one block east to **Teatro Victoria Eugenia**, inaugurated in 1912. At the top of the columns, look for sculptures depicting tragedy, comedy, drama and opera.

5 Belle Époque Hotel

Next to the theatre is the **Hotel Maria Cristina**, a wonderful example of belle époque architecture designed by Charles Mewes, the architect responsible for the Ritz hotels in Paris and London. It opened its doors in 1912, and the first guest was Queen María Cristina. Pop into the lobby, or browse the items on sale at Lukas Gourmet Shop.

6 Grand Cathedral

Follow the river upstream (south) to Puente de María Cristina and then walk west to reach **Catedral del Buen Pastor de San Sebastián**, the towering city cathedral. Built from slate and sandstone quarried from Monte Igueldo, the cathedral was consecrated in 1897 and has a 75m-high bell tower.

7 Waterside Cocktail

Head north along Calle de Easo and find your way to the Paseo de la Concha promenade and the **Real Club Náutico de San Sebastián** (San Sebastián's Nautical Club), built in a rationalist style in 1929. Stop for a drink at **Gu** (p130), or head to the beach.

EXPERIENCES

See the Emblematic Wind Comb

SCULPTURE

MAP: 1 P118 **A4**

San Sebastián's most celebrated artist is Eduardo Chillida (1924–2002), whose work explores shapes and spaces and how they interact with their surroundings.

At the western end of Playa de Ondarreta, look for his work **Peine del Viento** (Wind Comb), composed of three large steel shapes anchored to rocks so that the incoming wind whips through them like a comb. On stormy days, waves crash between the rocks and add to the drama. The work was installed in 1977 and has since become a symbol of the city. It's a 2km walk (30 minutes each way) from Playa de la Concha.

Learn to Make *Pintxos*

COOKING COURSE

MAP: 2 P118 **H2**

If you've developed a taste for *pintxos* (Basque tapas) and other Basque dishes, you can learn to make them yourself at **Mimo Bite The Experience** (mimo.eus). Classes take place every morning, each with a different theme: Spanish cooking (learn to make paella), traditional Basque cuisine and *pintxos*. There are also classes which include a trip to the market and preparation of a seasonal dish. The experience lasts five hours and includes lunch with wine (per person €195). Check the website to see the current schedule and to book.

You can also book a guided **food tour**, which includes five *pintxos* and five drinks (per adult €145). Children are welcome (there are reduced prices for kids, depending on their age).

Get Some Thalassotherapy at La Perla

SPA

MAP: 3 P118 **E4**

The healing powers of the ocean are harnessed at **La Perla** (la-perla.net), a seawater spa right on Playa de la Concha. La Perla's indoor thalassotherapy circuit (2/3/5 hours €35/40/50) comprises a hydrotherapy pool with seawater jets, as well as steam baths, ice fountains, saunas, cold plunge

MARÍA CRISTINA & THE BELLE ÉPOQUE

As you explore San Sebastián, you might find yourself wondering who María Cristina was, for whom the city's grandest hotel and most ornate bridge are named. Born in Austria in 1858, María Cristina married King Alfonso XII of Spain in 1879. In the late 19th century, Queen María Cristina (by then a widow) chose San Sebastián as the royal summer home, and **Palacio Miramar** was built as her house. Examples of belle époque architecture from the time include **La Perla**, **Koldo Mitxelena Kulturunea**, the **Ayuntamiento** and the **Funicular Railway**.

TRADITIONAL BASQUE MUSIC

While you're in the Basque Country, listen out for music played using traditional Basque musical instruments, such as the *alboka* (single-reed woodwind instrument), *txistu* (three-holed wooden pipe), *ttun-ttun* (six-stringed instrument named for the sound it makes) and *txalaparta* (a wooden percussion instrument that sounds similar to a xylophone). Learn more about these instruments and Basque musical traditions at the **San Telmo Museoa** (p101) in Parte Vieja. If you are interested in learning to play, head to **Erviti** (p131), which publishes Basque music scores and sells instruments.

pools and seawater showers. The jacuzzi and relaxation areas have views of La Concha bay and Isla de Santa Clara.

Book sessions online in advance. You need to bring a swimming cap or buy one at reception. You can also book treatments, such as seaweed wraps (€45) and seawater whirlpool baths (€41).

Catch an Exhibition at Koldo Mitxelena Kulturunea — CULTURAL CENTRE

MAP: 4 P118 **G4**

Set in a grand belle époque building dating from the 1890s, **Koldo Mitxelena Kulturunea** (kmk.gipuzkoa.eus) is a cultural centre with a packed lineup of art exhibitions, book launches, discussions and more. Check the website to see what's on. The centre is closed on Sundays and Mondays.

Don't miss the galleries downstairs, which mount free, thought-provoking exhibitions. The centre is named after Koldo Mitxelena, a writer and linguist and one of the great champions of creating a unified Basque language.

Watch a Performance at Teatro Victoria Eugenia — THEATRE

MAP: 5 P118 **H1**

Inaugurated in 1912, **Teatro Victoria Eugenia** (victoriaeugenia.eus) is one of Donostia-San Sebastián's landmark buildings. To see the extravagant marble foyer and the gilded theatre auditorium, you need to attend a performance. The theatre hosts an array of operas, concerts and dance performances. Check the website to see what's on, or ask at the on-site ticket office.

Surf the Ola de Tenis at Ondarreta — SURFING

MAP: 6 P118 **A4**

If you are an experienced surfer, San Sebastián's best wave is the *ola del tenis* (the tennis wave – it's by the tennis club), also known as the *muro de Ondarreta* (the Ondaretta wall). The wave is beneath Monte Igueldo at the far western end of **Playa de Ondarreta**, the western extension of Playa de la Concha.

The views are beautiful, and it's a fun wave to surf, but you can only surf it at high tide. Hire surfboards from **Club Deportivo Fortuna** (p120). In Gros, Pukas Surf Eskola also rents gear and is a good place to ask about tides and the swell.

Enjoy the Views at Jardines de Miramar

PARK

MAP: 7 P118 **B5**

Located between Playa de la Concha and Playa de Ondarreta with views of both, the grassy lawns of the **Jardines de Miramar** slope gently down to the ocean. The landscaped park is a scenic place to catch some sun or have a picnic with a view beside the magnificent **Palacio Miramar** (MAP: 8 P118 **B4**; miramar.eus), built in 1893 for **Queen María Cristina** (p126). Trees in the park include cork oaks, cherry trees, hazel pines, bitter orange trees and two pyramid-shaped yews. The flowerbeds are a riot of colours.

The summer 'cottages' of the British royal family inspired the palace, which was designed by English architect Selden Womun. In front of the house, look for the sculpture *Five Plates Counter Clockwise* by American artist Richard Serra. Nearby are further sculptures by Eduardo Chillida.

The building's interior is generally closed to the public – unless you decide to get married there.

Check Out Miramar's Beachside Art

PUBLIC ART

MAP: 9 P118 **B4**

The Jardines de Miramar extend over the rocky crag that separates the beaches of Playa de la Concha and Playa de Ondarreta, known as the Pico del Loro (the Parrot's Beak). At low tide, it's possible to walk along the sand from one beach to the other, but the beaches are also linked by a pedestrian tunnel. The tunnel walls have been transformed by the artwork *MiramArt* (*ItsasArte* in Basque), which depicts an underwater world. It looks particularly magical when lit up at night.

Above the tunnel, near the 'beak' of the Pico del Loro, look for Eduardo Chillida's sculpture **Abrazo** *(Embrace)*. Walk east along the Playa de la Concha promenade to see Chillida's **Monumento a Fleming** (MAP: 10 P118 **C4**; *Monument to Fleming*), a granite piece that was installed in 1991. It was created in 1955 to commemorate the death of Alexander Fleming, the biologist who discovered penicillin. The style is inspired by traditional Basque funeral steles.

See p118 for map of locations

Best Places for...

€ Budget €€ Midrange €€€ Top End

Eating

Pintxos

Altuna €
11 F4
Near Playa de la Concha, this chic bar serves freshly shucked oysters and inventive *pintxos*. *7.30-10.30pm Mon-Wed, 1-3.30pm & 7.30-10.30pm Thu-Sat*

Antonio Bar - Bergara3 €
12 H2
Serves highly rated, cooked-to-order *pintxos*, including battered squid and ham croquettes. *9am-11pm Mon-Thu, to midnight Fri & Sat; antoniobar.com*

Casa Valles €
13 H4
This timber-panelled local institution serves some of the neighbourhood's best *pintxos* beneath hanging hams. *11.30am-4pm & 6.30-11pm Tue-Sat, to 4.30pm Sun; barvalles.com*

Rojo y Negro €
14 F3
Come here to feast on *pintxos* washed down with cider or *txakoli* wine. It's also a good place for breakfast or brunch. *7am-1am; rojoynegro berri.com*

Basque Food

Narru €€€
15 G3
Showcases traditional Basque cooking using market ingredients. There's also a bar serving *pintxos* and plates. *12.30-4pm & 7.30-11pm; narru.es*

Antonio - Bergara3 €€€
see 12 H2
Below the bar, the small downstairs restaurant at Antonio's serves dishes like porcini mushrooms with egg yolk and foie gras. *1-3.30pm & 7-11pm Mon-Sat; antoniobar.com*

Kata.4 €€
16 H2
Feast on oysters, refined *pintxos*, or restaurant dishes like scallops or Iberian pork cheeks. *8am-4pm Mon, to 11.30pm Tue-Thu, 8am-12.30am Fri, from 10am Sat; kata4.com*

Rekondo €€€
17 A4
This elegant restaurant, on the way up Monte Igueldo, has wonderful views and an excellent wine cellar. *1.15-3.30pm & 8.30-10.30pm Thu-Mon; rekondo.com*

Fusion

Amelia €€€
18 F4
The menu at this two-Michelin-starred restaurant blends traditional Basque with Italian and Japanese influences. *7-8.30pm Wed & Thu, 1-2.30pm & 7-8.30pm Fri & Sat; ameliarestaurant.com*

Sukaldean Aitor Santamaría €€€
19 F4
Chef Aitor Santamaría offers Japanese and Basque-inspired sushi, as well as fish dishes and grilled meat. *1.30-3.30pm & 8.30-11pm Mon & Thu-Sun, 1.30-3.30pm Sun; sukaldeanaitorsanta maria.com*

Italian

Da Filippo €€€
20 H5
This contemporary restaurant serves beautifully presented bowls of ravioli and other Italian dishes. *1.30-5pm & 7.30-9.30pm Fri-Tue; da-filippo.com*

Cafes & Ice Cream

Botanika €
21 H3
A great spot for coffee or a smoothie with tomato toast or cake. *9am-5pm Mon, to 11pm Wed & Thu, to midnight Fri & Sat, to 6pm Sun; kafebotanika.eus*

Cafe de la Concha €€€
22 E4
In an art deco building in a prime beachside location, Cafe de la Concha serves beach-cafe fare (breakfasts, salads, burgers) and more gourmet mains. *9am-midnight; cafedelaconcha.com*

Arnoldo Heladería €
23 G2
In business since 1935, Arnoldo makes some of San Sebastián's best ice cream. The Calle Garibai store is one of seven branches in the city. *8am-11pm Mon-Thu, to 1am Fri-Sun; arnoldoheladeria.com*

Drinking

Coffee

Old Town Coffee
24 G4
Old Town roasts its own beans and offers a variety of brewing techniques. Also serves pastries and avocado toast. *8am-6pm Mon-Sat, to 1pm Sun; oldtowncoffeeroasters.com*

Somos
25 A5
This coffee shop and bakery serves breakfast, brunch and pastries baked in-house. *8.30am-3.30pm Tue-Sat, to 1.30pm Sun; somoskafe.com*

Cocktails & Dancing

Gu
26 F2
Glorious beach views extend from this waterfront cocktail bar in the 1929 Real Club Náutico de San Sebastián building. *5-10.30pm Mon & Wed, to 11pm Thu-Sun; gusansebastian.com*

Pokhara
27 H4
Relax with a cocktail during the week, or come for the weekend DJ sessions and live music. *9am-2am Mon-Fri, from 3pm Sat & Sun*

Bataplán Disco
28 E4
For beachside partying, head to this seafront club. In summer, you can warm up with a drink on the terrace. *noon-5.30am Thu, to 6am Fri & Sat; bataplandisco.com*

Bars

Drop
29 H4
Head here to get to grips with the local beer, with a range of Basque and international brews on tap and in bottles. *6pm-midnight Sun-Thu, to 4am Fri & Sat*

Museo del Whisky
30 G1
This atmospheric bar is full of bottles of Scotland's finest whiskies, as well as a museum's worth of knickknacks. *3.30pm-3.30am Mon-Sat*

Shopping

Food & Drink

Chocolates de Mendaro
31 H2
This famed chocolatier has been around since

850 and is still run by he Saint-Gerons family. *0am-1.30pm & 4.30-8pm Mon-Fri, 10am-1.30pm Sat; chocolatesde mendaro.com*

Elkano 1 Gaztagune

32 G1

More than 40 different artisan cheeses fill this aromatic little timber-lined shop. Most are from the Basque Country, including the owner's own sheep cheeses. *10am-2pm & 4.30-8pm Tue-Sat; elkano1.com*

Lukas Gourmet Shop

33 H2

This gourmet shop is where people with an appreciation of fine food and wine do their shopping. *9am-8pm Mon-Fri, 10am-2pm & 3-8pm Sat, 10am-2pm Sun; lukas-gourmet.com*

Mercado San Martín

34 G3

A modern food market with butchers, fishmongers, greengrocers, florists and bakeries (the hot, savoury pastries make great on-the-go snacks). *8am-8pm Mon-Sat; sanmartinmerkatua.com*

Fashion

Loreak Mendian

35 G2

This Basque label sells affordable fashion for men and women, everything from t-shirts and hoodies to dresses and sweaters. *10.30am-8pm Mon-Sat; loreak mendian.com*

Goiuri

36 G4

For statement-making swimwear, head to Goiuri, which stocks Australian brands of bikinis and one-piece swimsuits. *10am-8pm Mon-Sat; goiuri.com*

Minimil

37 G2

As the name suggests, Basque designer Contxu Uzkudun has a minimalist aesthetic, favouring a neutral palette and clean-cut designs. The label is now run by her daughters. *10.30am-8pm Mon-Sat; minimil.es*

Accessories

Anhelo

38 A5

Run by two sisters, this shop sells jewellery and accessories, including beautiful headpieces, as well as perfumes and candles. *10am-7pm Mon-Fri, to 1.30pm Sat; anhelo.es*

Box

39 H3

San Sebastián's architecture and landscapes are referenced in the designs of the leather bags here. *4-7.30pm Mon, 10am-1pm & 4-7.30pm Tue-Sat; boxsansebastian.com*

Music & Stationery

Erviti

40 H2

Established in 1875, Erviti sells musical instruments (including traditional Basque instruments) and publishes Basque musical scores. *10am-1.30pm & 4-7.30pm Mon-Fri, 10am-1.30pm Sat; erviti.com*

Tamayo

41 G1

If you need stationery or simply enjoy visiting art-supply stores, pop into Tamayo, in business since 1914. *9.30am-1.30pm & 4.30-8pm Mon-Fri, 10am-1.30pm & 5-8pm Sat; tamayo.es*

Perfume

Perfumería Benegas

42 G2

Founded in 1908, Benegas stocks SSirimiri perfumes, with fragrances inspired by the grassy mountains, flowers, sea and drizzle of San Sebastián. *10am-1.30pm & 4-7.30pm Mon-Sat; perfumeriabenegas.com*

See p140
for eating, drinking and shopping listings

Explore Donostia-San Sebastián Gros

The neighbourhood of Gros has a youthful energy and a lively surf scene. Altogether more laid-back than its neighbours across the river, Gros has several contemporary galleries that support emerging artists, as well as independent shops. Aside from its long surfing beach, the neighbourhood's main attractions are the Tabakalera (a former tobacco factory turned cultural centre) and the Kursaal, an unusual contemporary architectural design that houses a concert venue and conference centre. Come nightfall, the bars of Calle Zabaleta are the place to be, especially for Thursday night's *pintxo-pote*, when a drink and *pintxo* (Basque tapa) are offered for a low fixed price.

Getting Around

Walking

The neighbourhood landmarks of the Kursaal, Playa de la Zurriola, Monte Ulia and Río Urumea make Gros easy to navigate on foot.

Bicycle

The cycle lanes that run alongside Río Urumea and Playa de la Zurriola make the area particularly pleasant to explore by bike.

Bus

San Sebastián's bus station is located near the Puente de María Cristina in Gros. It's a 15-minute walk to the Parte Vieja and a 0-minute walk to Plaza de Gipuzkoa.

Puente de María Cristina (p137)
LVARO GERMAN VILELA/SHUTTERSTOCK ©

★

THE BEST

PINTXOS Bergara Bar (p140)

ARCHITECTURE Kursaal (p139)

PARK Parque de Cristina Enea (p137)

CULTURAL Tabakalera (p135)

DESIGN SHOP Arteuparte (p138)

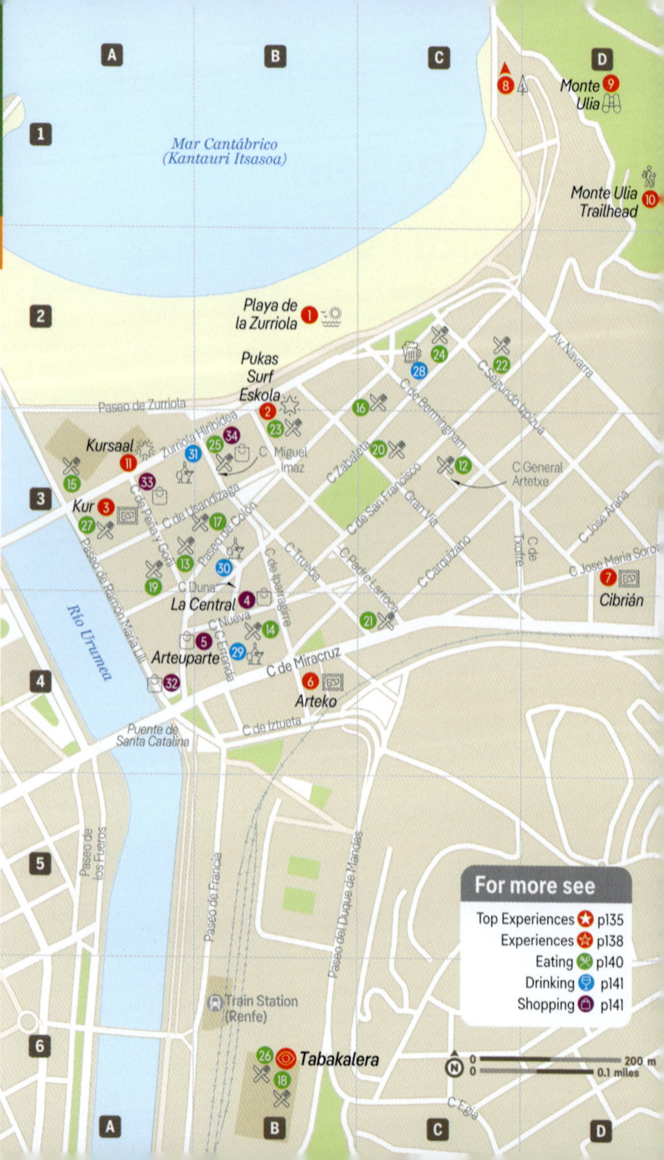
Mar Cantábrico (Kantauri Itsasoa)
Monte Ulia
Monte Ulia Trailhead
Playa de la Zurriola
Pukas Surf Eskola
Paseo de Zurriola
Kursaal
Zurriola Hiribidea
C Miguel Imaz
Kur
C de Peña y Goñi
C de Usandizaga
Paseo de Colón
C Duna
La Central
C Nueva
C Etxenea
Arteuparte
C de Ipatragirre
C Trueba
C Zabaleta
C de San Francisco
Gran Vía
C Padre Larroca
C Carquizano
C de Bermingham
C Segundo Izpizua
Av Navarra
C General Artetxe
C de Txofre
C Jose Arana
C Jose María Soroa
Cibrián
C de Miracruz
Arteko
C de Iztueta
Paseo de Ramón María Lili
Río Urumea
Puente de Santa Catalina
Paseo de los Fueros
Paseo de Francia
Paseo del Duque de Mandas
Train Station (Renfe)
Tabakalera
C Egia
For more see
Top Experiences p135
Experiences p138
Eating p140
Drinking p141
Shopping p141
200 m
0.1 miles

★ TOP EXPERIENCE

Tabakalera

Occupying a large, beautifully reconfigured tobacco factory dating from 1913, **Tabakalera** (tabakalera.eus) – the International Centre for Contemporary Culture – is a hub for the arts and cultural enterprises. Its various spaces include galleries, co-working offices, cafes, a meditation room and an arthouse cinema.

MAP P134 **B6**

Art

In the ground floor atrium hangs *Kuboa* (2020) by Argentinian artist Julio Le Parc. Created by Le Parc for the Tabakalera, the work comprises 2660 pieces of suspended polished stainless steel that gently move and reflect the light.

Head to the 1st-floor reception to find out what's on. The centre's four gallery spaces host temporary exhibitions featuring themes like fashion, photography, media and architecture. Most have tie-in events, such as guided tours, talks or performances. Admission is free.

Community Spirit

Tabakalera always has something interesting going on. Walk through the spaces and you might see teenagers rehearsing dance routines on a landing or a room packed with sewing machines and piles of clothes that turns out to be a workshop for people learning to upcycle their old gear. It's a good place to come on a rainy day, to catch a film at the cinema or settle down with a book in the ground-floor **Taba Cafe** (p141).

Rooftop Views

Head to the 5th floor to access a rooftop terrace with outstanding views. On the same floor, **LABe Restaurant** (p140) has its own rooftop seating.

PLANNING TIP

Tabakalera is closed on Monday. Free guided tours of the building in Spanish and Basque are offered on alternate weekends. Sign up online in advance.

Scan this QR code for cinema screening times and current exhibitions.

WALKING TOUR

Walk Gros

From watching surfers to admiring the architecture of two incredible arts venues, this walk captures the vibe of Gros. On the way, you'll stroll the banks of the Río Urumea, which separates Gros from the Parte Vieja and the New Town, before ending your walk in a beautifully landscaped park complete with peacocks.

START	END	LENGTH
Playa de la Zurriola	Parque de Cristina Enea	2.5km; one hour

1 Surfers' Beach

Start at **Playa de la Zurriola**, a sandy beach with breaks that attract surfers year-round. Pause to watch them paddle out to the swell by the claw-shaped wave breaker. You might see people playing volleyball on the sand.

2 Landmark Architecture

Walk west along the promenade to reach the **Kursaal**, the neighbourhood's most striking building. Opened in 1999, it serves as a cultural and conference centre. The construction consists of two cubes made of translucent glass with LED lights and was designed to represent two beached rocks. Walk around the outside of the building to get a good look.

3 Boutiques & Bars

Turn down Zurriola Hiribidea and then right onto pedestrianised Peña y Goñi, lined with restaurants, bars with outdoor tables, and boutiques. Bear right onto Paseo Colón. At Calle Berria, take a short detour to browse the art and clothes at **Arteuparte**.

4 Riverside Stroll

Cross Plaza Euskadi. Walk along the elegant riverside promenade Paseo del Urumea, passing sculptures and colourful flowerbeds, to reach **Puente de María Cristina**. The bridge was completed in 1905. Note the 18m-tall ornate obelisks topped with gilded sculptures of mounted horses.

5 Cultural Centre

Follow signs over the footbridge across the train tracks to reach **Tabakalera**, the former tobacco factory converted into a vast cultural centre. Walk around the building to get a sense of its scale.

6 Landscaped Park

The beautiful, landscaped **Parque de Cristina Enea** has shaded paths, duck ponds and grassy lawns patrolled by preening peacocks. It was once the summer residence of the Duke and Duchess of Mandas. Inside the park grounds, take a look at the pink Palacio del Duque de Mandas, which was their house and is now an environmental resource centre.

7 Towering Trees

Many of the plants and trees in the park are labelled. In the centre of the park (on the slope above the pond), look for the magnificent 30m-tall **Lebanese cedar tree**, planted in around 1864.

Explore Donostia-San Sebastián New Town

Aside from its fabulous food, Donostia-San Sebastián's other great draw is its beachside setting. Playa de la Concha and neighbouring Playa de Ondarreta offer golden sands, sheltered swimming and excellent people-watching. The New Town, also known as Centro Romántico, has the city's most notable belle époque architecture. It dates from the early 20th century when Queen María Cristina made San Sebastián her summer home, and the city became popular with aristocrats. But this neighbourhood is not only home to artistic creations of decades past. Eduardo Chillida's *Peine del Viento*, sculptures that have come to represent the city, mark the neighbourhood's westernmost point.

Getting Around

Walking

The New Town is easy to navigate on foot, especially along the 2km-long waterfront promenade.

Bicycle

Cycle paths run throughout the neighbourhood, including along the coast between Alderdi Eder park and Monte Igueldo. Hire a bike from Sanse Bikes or Darwin Rentals.

Bus

Bus 16 runs from the city centre to the base of Monte Igueldo via Playa de la Concha. Several bus routes leave from Plaza de Gipuzkoa.

Paseo de la Concha (p121)

★

THE BEST

BEACH Playa de la Concha (p120)

SPA La Perla (p126)

VIEWS Monte Igueldo (p122)

RESTAURANT Amelia (p129)

COOKING COURSE Mimo Bite The Experience (p126)

EXPERIENCES

Catch Waves or Hang Out on the Sand at Playa de la Zurriola

BEACH

MAP: 1 P134 B2

Stretching for 800m in front of Gros, **Playa de la Zurriola** (known locally as Zurri) has some excellent waves that draw surfers from near and far. It's a superb place to hang out and take in the local scene of volleyball, football and surf action. Swimming is best when there's no swell.

You can hire gear and book lessons at **Pukas Surf Eskola** (MAP: 2 P134 B2; eskola.pukassurf.com). A three-hour weekend course costs €75, and longer courses are also available.

The best conditions for beginners are low tide near the breakwater at the western end of the beach. Early mornings are generally a good time because it's usually less windy. The biggest waves are from September to April.

Discover Gros' Galleries

ART

MAP: 3 P134 A3

Gros is home to some of San Sebastián's best galleries and art shops. Allow about an hour to walk among them and view the exhibitions.

Start at **Kur** (kurgallery.com; closed on Sundays), which hosts exhibitions of work by exciting contemporary artists.

Spread over two floors, **La Central** (MAP: 4 P134 B4; lacentralart gallery.com) is a contemporary art gallery in an industrial-style space, with some affordable pieces and prints. Nearby, **Arteuparte** (MAP: 5 P134 A4; arteuparte.com; closed Sunday) is the perfect place to browse for graphic art prints, ceramics, textiles and fashion.

Stop by to see the work in **Arteko** (MAP: 6 P134 B4; artekogallery.com; closed Sunday to Tuesday) and then stroll down to **Cibrián** (MAP: 7 P134 D3; cibrian.eu; closed Monday), which displays the work of emerging artists.

A CITY OF CULINARY STARS

Edible river stones, cod gel and seaweed foam: eating in one of San Sebastian's multi-Michelin-star restaurants is an experience you'll never forget. Currently, three restaurants in or near San Sebastián hold three Michelin stars: **Arzak** (arzak.es), **Akelaŕe** (akelarre.net) and **Martín Berasategui Restaurant** (martinberasategui.com). All feature prominently in lists of the world's best restaurants. The chefs at these places are culinary alchemists who combine art and science to concoct dishes in their cooking laboratories. Expect to pay at least €200 per person (excluding wine). You need to reserve a table months in advance.

Watch the Sunset in Sagüés

VIEWPOINT

MAP: 8 P134 C1

San Sebastián has endless places to watch the setting sun, but for the best sunset of all, head to the Sagüés neighbourhood at the far eastern end of Playa de la Zurriola.

From the Kursaal, it's a 800m (10-minute) walk along the seafront to a beachside children's playground and Sagüés skate park. Continue along the path to **Paloma de la Paz** (*Dove of Peace*), a sculpture by Basque artist Nestor Basterretxea (1924–2024). The benches here are the perfect place to watch the sunset.

Climb Monte Ulia

HIKING

MAP: 9 P134 D1

At the eastern end of Playa de la Zurriola stands **Monte Ulia** (235m), traversed by several scenic hiking trails. Allow two hours for the 5.5km summit loop hike (the SL-GI 33 Uliari bira route), including rest stops. Wear hiking boots or sturdy shoes. The path gets slippery in wet weather.

The trickiest part to navigate is finding the **trailhead** (MAP: 10 P134 D1). It begins at the top of the steps leading uphill from Calle de Zemoria. This is also the starting point for the coastal hike to Pasaia. From the trailhead, both routes are signed. The summit loop hike is indicated with green and white markings.

The trail passes through woodland before emerging out to ocean views. Look out for the moss-covered **Peña del Ballenero**, a former whale-watching lookout point. At the top of Monte Ulia is a children's playground and picnic tables (this area is also accessible by road).

Catch a Concert at the Kursaal

LIVE PERFORMANCE

MAP: 11 P134 A3

An energetic and exciting array of performances are staged at the **Kursaal** (kursaal.eus), a concert venue and conference centre that is also an architectural landmark.

Shows include everything from symphonic concerts, live bands and musicals to dance performances and rock shows. Check the website for details of upcoming events and to buy tickets.

In September, the Kursaal hosts screenings during the **San Sebastián International Film Festival** (sansebastianfestival.com). It's also where the festival's opening and closing galas and award ceremonies take place. Buy cinema tickets online or at one of the dedicated festival box offices, which are listed on the website.

LISTINGS

Best Places for...

See p134 for map of locations

€ Budget €€ Midrange €€€ Top End

Eating

Pintxos & Plates

Bergara Bar €
12 C3
Serves some of the city's best *pintxos*. Try the *txalupa* (a puff-pastry boat topped with mushrooms and prawns). *10.30am-11pm Mon-Sat, from 11am Sun; pinchos bergara.es*

Bodega Donostiarra €
13 A3
Crowds pack in for *pintxos*, including tortilla with Roquefort or cod, battered hake, and grilled octopus. *9am-11pm Mon-Fri, 10am-midnight Sat; bodegadonostiarra.com*

Gerald's Bar €€
14 B4
The menu changes daily but usually includes dishes like pork chops, and fried aubergine with marinated cucumber and labneh cheese. *1-5pm & 7.30pm-1am Tue-Sun; geraldsbar.eu*

Contemporary Basque

Muka €€€
15 A3
In a minimalist dining room at the Kursaal with views of the river, Muka serves unpretentious modern Basque cuisine. *noon-11pm Mon-Sun; muka.eus*

Galerna €€€
16 C2
At Galerna, chef Rebeka Barainka offers seasonal tasting menus of impeccably prepared and presented dishes made with local ingredients. *1-8pm; galernajanedan.com*

Ikaitz €€€
17 B3
Expect traditional Basque dishes with modern touches at this family-run restaurant. *1-3.30pm & 8.30-10pm Wed & Thu, to 10.30pm Fri, 1.30-3.30pm & 8.30-10.30pm Sat; restauranteikaitz.com*

LABe Restaurant €€
18 B6
Enjoy breakfast, lunch or a cocktail with fabulous views at Tabakalera's restaurant. *10am-5pm Wed-Sun; labe-dgl.com*

Fusion

Topa Sukaldería €€
19 A3
The menu features Basque dishes with South American influences. *1-3pm & 7.30-10pm Sun-Thu, to 10.30pm Fri & Sat; topasukalderia.com*

Casa 887 €€€
20 C3
Brazilian chef Antonio Carlos Fountoura infuses his creative plates with flavours from all over the world. *8-11pm Tue, 1-4pm & 8-11pm Wed-Sat, 1-4pm Sun; grupo887.com*

Vegetarian & Health Food

Mapa Verde €€
21 C4
All the dishes at this popular lunch spot are vegan. *12.30-3.30pm Mon-Fri, to 4pm Sat*

Alabama Cafe €€
22 C2
This health-food cafe serves smoothies, breakfasts and poke bowls, with plenty of vegan and gluten-free options. *8am-9pm Tue-Fri, from 8.30am Sat & Sun; alabamacafe.es*

Enxalao €

23 B3

Head here for healthy breakfasts, salads, super bowls, poke bowls and vegan options, as well as smoothies, coffee and desserts. *9.30am-4.30pm; enxalao.com*

Cafes

La Guinda €€

24 C2

This little cafe serves breakfasts and international dishes like burgers, vegetarian lasagne and tacos. *8.30am-5pm Tue & Wed, to 11pm Thu, to 11.30pm Fri, from 9am Sat, 9am-5pm Sun; laguindadelicoffee.com*

Loaf €

25 B3

Serves freshly baked bread, cakes and cookies. A perfect post-surf breakfast spot. *9am-8pm; theloaf.eus*

Taba Cafe €

26 B6

On the ground floor of Tabakalera, this cafe has various counters serving high-quality coffee, beer, *pintxos*, pastries and pizzas. *9am-11pm; taba.eus*

Simona Specialty Coffee Club €

27 A3

Head here for speciality coffee, brunch (Turkish eggs, granola, pastrami sandwiches) and cakes. *9am-7pm (kitchen to 3pm); simonacoffeeclub.com*

Drinking

Craft Beer

Mala Gissona Beer House

28 C2

Serves craft beers from the Mala Gissona brewery in Irun alongside other brews. *1pm-midnight Mon-Fri, noon-1.30am Sat, to 10.30pm Sun; malagissona.beer*

Bar Desy

29 B4

Craft beer and delectable *pintxos* make a killer combination at this tiny bar. Try the mini burgers. *6am-11pm Mon-Sat*

Bars

La Gintonería Donostiarra

30 B3

This corner cocktail bar specialises in gin, and behind the bar are bottles from all over the world. *8pm-1am Wed & Thu, 7pm-2am Fri, from 5pm Sat, 7pm-1am Sun; facebook.com/LaGintoneriaDonostiarra*

Ondarra

31 A3

Across the road from Playa de la Zurriola, Ondarra draws a chilled-out surf crowd. *11am-10.30pm Sun-Thu, to 1am Fri & Sat; ondarra.eus*

Shopping

Fashion & Accessories

Pas Si Simple

32 A4

Browse this boutique for chic but casual dresses, skirts, t-shirts, bags and shoes. *10.30am-1.30pm & 4.30-8pm Mon-Fri, 11am-2pm & 4.30-8pm Sat; passisimple.es*

Soule

33 A3

This womenswear boutique is a great place to hit up for soft linen shirts, oversized sweaters and dresses. *10.30am-1.30pm & 4.30-8pm Mon-Sat; soule.es*

Hawaii

34 B3

Seafront surf shop selling wetsuits and surfboards, as well as t-shirts, shorts and caps. Also has gear to rent. *10am-8pm; hawaiidonostia.com*

★ WORTH A TRIP

Chillida Leku

View more than 40 sculptures by local artist Eduardo Chillida at this outdoor garden museum, which Chillida envisaged as a space where people could walk through the sculptures like trees in a forest. A 16th-century farmhouse gallery houses further works.

PLANNING TIP
The museum is 7km south of San Sebastián's city centre. Catch bus BU05 from Plaza Zubieta (15 minutes). Allow about two hours to look around.

Scan this QR code for opening hours and prices.

Viewing the Sculptures

Chillida (1924–2002) referred to himself as a sculptor of emptiness, and his work explored shapes and spaces and how they interact with their surroundings. In 1983, Chillida and his wife, Pilar Belzunce, began work creating the 11-hectare **garden** (museochillidaleku.com; adult/child €14/7) in which more than 40 of the sculptor's works now stand, rooted in nature.

Start your visit in the Sala Pilar, where you can see old photos and learn about Chillida's life. A video shows Chillida's work processes and how he forged his steel sculptures. Don't miss the sketch by Chillida of his wife's face and hands.

Spread out in the grassy lawns outside, Chillida's pieces appear to emerge from the ground. There is no particular order in which to see them. Chillida said the viewer should be guided by their intuition and follow the works' 'scent'. You can also touch the outdoor sculptures – mostly made of steel and granite – to feel the texture of the materials.

Chillida worked with different themes to create families of numbered sculptures. Look for *Peine del viento XVII* (Wind Comb XVII), *Lo profundo es el aire XVII* (How Profound is the Air XVII). *Gora bera III* (Up Down III) sits in the centre of a peaceful meditation garden.

LUIS PIZARRO RUIZ/SHUTTERSTOCK ©

Restored Farmhouse

The impeccably restored 16th-century stone-walled Zabalaga farmhouse (pictured) is now a gallery space housing some of Chillida's more delicate sculptures, including pieces made with alabaster. The space is also used for temporary exhibitions of work by other artists.

The pieces inside are displayed on the ground and mezzanine floor beneath old oak beams. Light pours in from large windows, which frame the sculptures in the grounds beyond.

Events

Check the website for upcoming events, such as summer solstice celebrations, outdoor film screenings, guided meditations and yoga sessions among the sculptures.

See p154 for eating and shopping listings

Explore
Pasaia & Hondarribia

East of Donostia-San Sebastián are two key maritime settlements, both in scenic locations. Pasaia is a historic port, made up of four distinct districts. The most appealing for visitors are Pasai San Pedro, with its fascinating whaling museum, and Pasai Donibane, which has cobbled streets and outstanding seafood restaurants. These two villages face each other on opposite sides of the river estuary, crossed by a small passenger ferry. It's possible to hike to Pasaia from San Sebastián via a scenic coastal trail. Further east, at the French border, Hondarribia has a walled *casco histórico* (historic centre) and a thriving food scene.

Getting Around

Walking

Hondarribia's *casco histórico* is pedestrianised. It's a 2km (25-minute) walk from the Casco to Playa de Hondarribia.

Bus

From Donostía-San Sebastián's Gipuzkoa Plaza, bus E09 goes to Pasai San Pedro (15 minutes), and buses E20 and E27 go to Hondarribia (52 minutes).

Ferry

A small passenger ferry makes the crossing between Pasai San Pedro and Pasai Donibane. In Hondarriba, boats for Hendaye in France leave every 15 minutes from Paseo Butrón.

Pasai Donibane
ALBERTO LOYO/SHUTTERSTOCK ©

THE BEST

MARITIME MUSEUM Albaola Foundation (p148)

BEACH Hendaye (p153)

BIKE RIDE Monte Jaizkibel (p152)

NIGHTLIFE Calle San Pedro (p153)

COASTAL HIKE Pasaia (p152)

HONDARRIBIA
A
B
C
D
1
2
3
4
5
6
0
400 m
0
0.2 miles
Kayak Basque Country 3
Playa de Hondarribia
Paseo Europa
C Higer Bidea
Minatera Ibilbidea
Enlargement
C Mabin Artzu
C Almirante Alonso
Paseo Butron Ibilbidea
Calle San Pedro 9
C Santiago
C Zuloaga
C Bernat Etxepare
Basoa Bike Shop 5
See Enlargement
SPAIN
FRANCE
Río Bidasoa
Hendaye 7
Paseo Butron Ibilbidea
Hendaye-Hondarribia Ferry 8
C Labreder
6
HONDARRIBIA
C Santiago
Paseo Bidasoa
C Sorroeta
LA MARINA
Lezo - Hondarribia Jaizkibel Gainetik
C Sabin Arana Gori
C San Nicolás
CASCO HISTÓRICO
C Harresilanda
C Minasoroeta
14
15
16
17
18
19
20
21
22
23
24
25
26
27
28
29
30
31

PASAIA
A
B
C
D
1
2
3
4
5
6
0 400 m
0 0.2 miles
Ría de Pasaia
Faro de la Plata
1
Albaola Foundation
4
PASAI DONIBANE
C Donibane
Plaza de Santiago
11
2
12
10
C Torreatze
PASAI SAN PEDRO
C San Pedro
C Arraunlari
C Arrandegi
TRINTXERPE
13
Av Euskadi
C Esnabide
Pasaiako Portuko Zeharbidea
OLETA
For more see
Top Experiences p148
Experiences p152
Eating p154
Shopping p155

★ TOP EXPERIENCE

Albaola Foundation

The Albaola Foundation is a fascinating maritime museum in Pasai San Pedro that charts the history of the area's whaling industry. The highlight of the foundation's exhibition is the life-size replica of the San Juan whaling ship constructed using the same techniques and materials that were used to build the original, which sank off the coast of Canada in 1565.

MAP P147 **C3**

Scan this QR code for opening hours or to book a guided tour.

Pasaia's Whaling Past

The **museum** (albaola.org; adult/child €10/7) occupies a prime location at the edge of the Oiartzun estuary. Whaling ships once sailed along this very channel at the start of their 6300km journey across the North Atlantic route to Newfoundland. Basque whalers would set off in March or April, their ship loaded with local cider, and arrive in early June, when the coast was free of ice.

Museum Exhibits

At the centre of the story is the *San Juan*, a galleon that sunk off the coast of Newfoundland in 1565. Models and explanatory panels describe the ship and illustrate how a team of Canadian underwater archaeologists discovered its wreck in 1978. Don't miss the small model of the *San Juan*.

MARK GREEN/SHUTTERSTOCK ©

ɫeconstruction

ılbaola's star attraction is the life-size (28m-long) econstruction of the *San Juan* that is being built ısing the same techniques and materials that were ısed to make the original. Even the oak trees used ɔr wood are felled in the traditional way. Watch he workers measuring planks and hammering ıails with wooden mallets as you walk around the hip from observation platforms, inhaling the smell f oak.

PLANNING TIP

The quayside area leading to the museum is not accessible by car. The nearest car park is a six-minute walk away in Pasai San Pedro.

WALKING TOUR

Walk Hondarribia's Casco Viejo

Hondarribia's walled historic centre, much of which dates from the 15th and 16th centuries, is a grid of atmospheric plazas, cobbled lanes, and houses with wooden eaves and wrought-iron balconies adorned with flowers. Discover the historic buildings as you wander the narrow streets.

START	END	LENGTH
Puerta de Santa María	Puerta de Santa María	1km; 40 minutes

1 Entering the Casco

Begin at **Puerta de Santa María**, one of the Casco's two original ateways. Guarding the gate is the ronze statue, *Hatxero*, of a Hond-rribian soldier wearing a bearskin at. Above the gate, look for the ity crest, crowned by the Virgin de Guadalupe. Go through the gate to ee stone and timber houses from enturies past.

2 Seafarers' Church

Valk up Calle Mayor to reach the **glesia de Santa María de la Asunción**, where for centuries ailors have prayed for a safe oyage. The church was built in combination of styles (Gothic, Renaissance and baroque) between he 15th and 18th centuries. Inside, y the door, look for two huge hell fonts held up by stone hands merging from the walls.

3 Historic Square

At the centre of the Casco is **Plaza de Armas**, a cobblestone square hat transports you back in time o the Middle Ages. Pop into the ourist office, housed in the former own hall. Helpful staff can give ou maps and tips.

4 Medieval Castle

Dominating the square is **Castillo de Carlos V**, built in 1190. Today it is a hotel, but for centuries, the castle hosted knights and kings. Its position atop the old town hill gave it a commanding view over the strategic Bidasoa estuary, which marks the border with France. Poke your head into the reception lobby to see the medieval interior.

5 Pretty Plaza

Walk down Calle San Nicolás and bear right to reach **Plaza de Gipuzkoa**, a scenic and peaceful square. Stop for a *pintxo* (Basque tapa) or plate in **Badia Taberna** (p154).

6 Historic Walls

Exit the Casco through **Puerta de San Nicolás**. From here, you can see the structure of the remarkably intact walls. Follow the path around the outside of the walls. Look for damage left by cannon balls in years gone by.

7 Defensive Bastion

As you walk back towards Puerta de Santa María, you pass the 16th-century **Baluarte de la Reina** (Queen's Bastion). Beneath the bastion is a tunnel; pop inside to see an old artillery platform.

EXPERIENCES

Hike the Coastal Trail from San Sebastián to Pasaia HIKING

MAP: 1 P147 C2

On the banks of the beautiful Oiartzun estuary are four waterside settlements collectively known as Pasaia. The area is an idyllic location for a seafood lunch. A wonderful way to get there is on foot via the coastal path from San Sebastián. Allow three hours for the 7.5km walk, plus time in Pasaia.

The trail begins at the eastern end of **Playa de la Zurriola** (p138), at the top of the steps leading from Calle de Zemoria up Monte Ulia. Once at the **Monte Ulia trailhead** (p139), the route is well signed.

Highlights include flysch formations in the cliffs, woodlands, wildflowers, sea views and the rocky cove of Playa de Murgita. From **Faro de la Plata** (a lighthouse), look down to the knife-like slit in the cliff face that allows boat access to the ports of Pasaia.

The walk ends at **Pasai San Pedro**, where you can visit the **Albaola Foundation** (p148).

Have a Seafood Lunch in Pasaia's Plaza de Santiago SQUARE

MAP: 2 P147 D4

From Pasai San Pedro, hop in the little boat (€1.85) that ferries passengers back and forth to Pasai Donibane, a cluster of green and white houses that lean out over the waters of a narrow natural port.

From the ferry pier, it's a five-minute walk to **Plaza de Santiago** for a seafood lunch. Tak[e] your pick of the **square's restaurants** (p154), which have wonderful views of the estuary. For a scenic post-lunch stroll, follow the coastal path towards the mouth of the estuary (1km, allow 30 minute[s] for the walk there and back).

You can catch the bus back to San Sebastián from Calle Esnabid[e] in Pasai San Pedro.

Go Paddling at Sunset KAYAKIN[G]

MAP: 3 P146 B1

From April to October, **Kayak Basque Country** (kayakbasquecountry.com) offers a range of kayaking excursions, including 1½ hour sunset paddles around the bay (per person €22). From June to September, you can also hire kayaks (€10 per hour) to explore on your own. Look for it at **Playa de Hondarribia**.

Ride a Bike Up Monte Jaizkibel CYCLIN[G]

MAP: 4 P147 D3

For the Basque Country's serious cyclists, the 9.8km climb up **Monte Jaizkibel** (547m) from Hondarribia has an almost mythical status.

Although it's not the region's most challenging climb, it's not one to take on unless you are a regular cyclist. The route has

THE NORTHERN ROUTE TO SANTIAGO

Though most pilgrims hike the Camino Frances through Pamplona and Logroño on their way to Santiago, an alternative route is the northern path, known as the Camino del Norte (Northern Way). The initial stages (214km, about eight days of hiking) pass through the Basque Country, offering stunning scenery but tough walking with plenty of hills. The Camino del Norte begins in Irun (adjacent to Hondarribia), passing the Santuario de Guadalupe. You can pick up the route in Hondarribia and hike as far as the Guadalupe hermitage (a 4km uphill climb).

an average gradient of 4.5% and climbs to 453m at its highest point. **Basoa Bike Shop** (MAP: 5 P146 B4; basoabike.com) rents good-quality mountain bikes and e-bikes (per hour/day €15/55); reserve ahead.

At 5km, the **Santuario de Guadalupe** (MAP: 6 P146 A5) hermitage marks the halfway point to the summit. Pop inside to see the shrine to the Virgin and hanging model ships. The picnic tables here are a good place to stop for a break. You can also drive here.

The road wends up Jaizkibel, a giant slab of rock topped with a ruined fortress. Enjoy the views from the top and the downhill ride back.

Allow two to three hours, depending on your cycling speed and rest stops.

Take the Ferry to France BOAT TRIP

MAP: 7 P146 D3

To dip your toes in French water, take the seven-minute ferry trip to the beach at **Hendaye**. Boats leave every 15 minutes from **Paseo Butrón** (MAP: 8 P146 C4; per person €2.50; jolaski.com).

Apart from nibbling on flaky croissants and other French cuisine, Hendaye's main attraction is its 3km-long stretch of white-sand beach, a 250m stroll north of the ferry dock. It's protected by a headland that ensures calm waters for swimming.

Discover the Bars of Calle San Pedro STREET

MAP: 9 P146 A3

The heart of Hondarribia's La Marina district is **Calle San Pedro**. This quaint pedestrian-only strip is flanked by traditional fishers' houses with facades painted bright green or blue, and wooden balconies cheerfully decorated with flower boxes. Many of the old buildings now contain *pintxo* bars and restaurants.

The street is lively at lunchtime, but it really gets going after dark. The pick of the *pintxo* bars is **Gran Sol** (p155).

LISTINGS

Best Places for...

See pp146-147 for map of locations

€ Budget €€ Midrange €€€ Top End

Eating

Around Pasaia

Casa Cámara €€€

MAP: 10 P147 **D4**

This sophisticated restaurant in Pasai Donibane serves seafood with sea views. *1.30-3pm Sun & Tue-Thu, 1.30-3pm & 8.30-10pm Fri & Sat; casacamara.com*

Yola Berri €€

MAP: 11 P147 **D4**

Sit in Plaza Santiago and snack on grilled cuttle-fish, prawns and other fresh seafood. *10am-6pm Tue-Thu, to 9pm Fri & Sat, to 7pm Sun*

Ziaboga Bistrot €€

MAP: 12 P147 **D4**

Take in the water views as you dine on crab-crusted hake fillet or squid cooked in its own ink. *11am-9pm Wed-Mon; ziabogabistrot.com*

Izkiña €€

MAP: 13 P147 **A5**

Try the *raciones* (full-plate servings) of fried calamari or anchovies at this Pasai San Pedro restaurant and bar. *11.30am-4pm Sun & Tue-Thu, 11.30am-4pm & 7-11pm Fri & Sat; restaurant eizkina.com*

Restaurants in Hondarribia

El Curry Verde €€

MAP: 14 P146 **B1**

Colourful vegetarian restaurant (with vegan options) serving breakfast and lunch, including Asian-inspired dishes. The outdoor tables overlook the marina. *9am-3.30pm Tue-Sun; elcurryverde.com*

Gastroteka Danontzat €€

MAP: 15 P146 **C6**

Chef Gorka Irisarri's fun approach to food combines beautifully prepared fresh ingre-dients with creative presentation and props. *noon-midnight Thu-Mon; gastrotekadanontzat.com*

Badia Taberna €€

MAP: 16 P146 **C5**

This little bar and restaurant in the *casco histórico* serves plates of fresh local ingredients, full of flavour. Excellent wine cellar too. *5-11pm Wed-Sat & Mon, from noon Sun; badiataberna.com*

Arroka Berri €€€

MAP: 17 P146 **A1**

Takes quality local produce and refines old-fashioned recipes with a dash of invention. It's in the hills, with garden seating. *1-3.30pm & 8.30-11pm; arrokaberri.es*

Cafes in Hondarribia

Amona Margarita €

MAP: 18 P146 **B4**

Bright, cheery cafe and bakery selling freshly baked bread, sandwiches and pastries. *7.30am-9pm Mon-Fri, from 8am Sat & Sun; amonamargarita.com*

Gaxen €

MAP: 19 P146 **B3**

This low-key local cafe is the place to go for good-value breakfasts and Basque pastries. *7.30am-1pm & 4-8pm*

Splash-Out Meals

Alameda €€€

MAP: 20 P146 **C6**

Serving creative takes on traditional Basque cuisine, Michelin-starred Alameda helped

Hondarribia become the culinary hot spot it is today. *1-3.30pm Sun, Wed & Thu, 1-3.30pm & 8-11pm Fri & Sat; restaurantealameda.net*

Laía Erretegia €€€

MAP: 21 P146 **B6**

The beef here is aged for 30 to 60 days before being grilled over charcoal. *1-3pm Mon-Fri, 1.30-3pm & 8.30-10pm Sat, 1.30-3pm Sun; laiaerretegia.com*

Asador Sutan €€€

MAP: 22 P146 **B6**

Located at the Hirutza *txakoli* winery, Sutan offers a short menu of barbecued meat and freshly caught fish and seafood. *1-3.30pm Sun & Tue-Fri, 1-3.30pm & 8-10pm Sat; sutan.eus*

La Hermandad de Pescadores €€€

MAP: 23 P146 **B3**

Housed in a traditional white-and-blue cottage, this Hondarribia institution serves an array of top-rate seafood. *1-3.30pm & 8-10.30pm Tue-Sat, 1-3.30pm Sun*

Pintxo Bars

Vinoteka Ardoka €

MAP: 24 P146 **A3**

Contemporary wine and *pintxos* bar in Hondarribia, serving local *txakoli* wine and a range of vermouths. *11.30am-3.30pm & 6-11.30pm Wed-Mon; ardokavinoteka.com*

Gran Sol €

MAP: 25 P146 **A3**

Head to this bar on Hondarribia's Calle San Pedro for exquisite, multi-award-winning *pintxos* as well as local wines and craft beers. *11am-3.30pm Sun & Tue-Thu, 11am-3.30pm & 7.30-10pm Fri & Sat; bargransol.com*

Itsaspe €

MAP: 26 P146 **A2**

On Calle San Pedro, Itsaspe's bar serves *pintxos* and *raciones*, including buckets of mussels to share. *10am-3.30pm & 8-11pm; restauranteitsaspe.com*

Shopping

Food & Drink

Conservas Hondarribia

MAP: 27 P146 **C5**

The produce at this deli is sourced from local suppliers: anchovies, cheeses, chocolate, cider, *txakoli* wines and more. *11am-2pm Wed-Fri, 10am-2pm & 3.30-7.30pm Sat & Sun; conservashondarribia.com*

Conservas Done Pedro

MAP: 28 P146 **B4**

This ship-like store sells beautifully packaged Done Pedro tinned sardines, anchovies and tuna. *10am-1.30pm & 4.30-8.30pm Mon-Fri, 10am-2pm & 4-8pm Sat, 10am-2pm Sun; donepedro.com*

Fashion & Accessories

Six Store

MAP: 29 P146 **B3**

Stocks clothes in colourful prints, accessories and shoes for women and men. There's a second branch in San Sebastián. *10am-2.30pm & 4-8pm*

Soule

MAP: 30 P146 **B3**

This local label produces sophisticated designs for women. This is the original store; there is another in San Sebastián. *10.30am-1.30pm & 4.30-8pm Mon-Sat; soule.es*

Homewares

Rosario Berrotarán

MAP: 31 P146 **B3**

With a photogenic storefront, this shop is packed with baskets, buckets and other fishing-related items, some of which make great souvenirs. *9.30am-1.30pm & 4.30-8pm Mon-Sat, 9.30am-1.30pm Sun*

Bilbao & San Sebastián Toolkit

Bilbao (p33)

Family Travel

Bilbao and Donostia-San Sebastián are family-friendly destinations with excellent transport and accommodation infrastructure, food to satisfy even the fussiest of eaters, and a good range of attractions that appeal to both adults and children.

Eating Out

Children are generally welcome at restaurants. If you are planning a meal in one of the region's top Michelin-starred places, check the policy for children when you book. Many restaurants offer a children's menu (*menú infantil*). At *pintxo* (Basque tapa) bars, the options are the same for adults and kids.

BEACHES

The beaches of the Basque coast are particularly appealing for families, thanks to sheltered areas for swimming. Lifeguards patrol beaches in Bizkaia and San Sebastián from 1 June to 30 September from 11am to 8pm.

Admission Fees

Most attractions offer free admission for children, but the cut-off age varies. For a few, including the Museo Guggenheim Bilbao, anyone under 18 gets in free. However, the age limit is usually lower. Some attractions, such as San Sebastián's Aquarium, offer free admission for kids under four and reduced-price tickets for children aged four to 14.

Babies

The right to breastfeed in public is protected by law and widely accepted. Most hotels have cots (*cunas*); request one when booking.

Public Transport

Children under six ride free on public transport in Bilbao and Donostia-San Sebastián.

Playgrounds

Children's playgrounds are all over Bilbao and San Sebastián, including in pretty much every city park and many squares. The newer ones have roofs to provide shade from the sun.

ZENOBILLIS/SHUTTERSTOCK ©

Accommodation

Bilbao and Donostia-San Sebastián have plenty of accommodation options but are so popular in summer that places book up in advance.

Where to stay if you love...

Belle Époque Buildings

Donostia-San Sebastián's New Town (p117) The widest range of accommodation options, including some of the best hotels in the city. Access to beaches. Surrounded by belle époque architecture, including the luxurious Hotel Maria Cristina (p125).

Bar-Hopping & Shopping

Bilbao's Old Town (p35) Lots of charm. Surrounded by lively *pintxo* bars, but can be noisy at night. The city's main sights are a walk or metro ride away.

Beaches & Coastal Hikes

Central Basque Coast (p85) Beautiful beaches right on your doorstep. Seafood restaurants and Basque culture. Coastal hiking nearby. Fills with holidaymakers in summer.

Pintxos & Nightlife

Donostia-San Sebastián's Parte Vieja (p99) Steps away from the city's best *pintxo* bars. Near Playa de la Concha and several key sights but feels touristy and gets crowded.

Architecture & Art

Bilbao New Town (p49) Good choice of hotels, including some with river views. Home to the city's best dining options. Puts you near Bilbao's best-known sights, including the Guggenheim.

OUR PICK

We love to stay in...

Gros (p133) This Donostia-San Sebastián neighbourhood has an arty vibe and a youthful feel. It's home to the city's best surfing beach and bar scene, as well as San Sebastián's most exciting new restaurants. It's cheaper and quieter than the Parte Vieja but just a short, scenic walk away.

HOW MUCH FOR A NIGHT IN

Hostel dorm room from **€25**

Midrange guest-house from **€90**

Boutique hotel from **€180**

Food, Drink & Nightlife

Allergies & Intolerances

People with allergies should take care when eating out, particularly at *pintxo* bars when you might not be certain of the ingredients. Always state your allergy clearly when ordering.

HOW TO SAY

I'm allergic to... Soy alérgico / alérgica a...
nuts los frutos secos
seafood los mariscos
dairy los lácteos
gluten gluten

> **?**
> **HOW TO ASK...**
> **Is this gluten free?**
> ¿Esto es libre de gluten?
> **Does this contain nuts?**
> ¿Esto tiene frutos secos?
> **Is there a vegan option?**
> ¿Hay opción vegana?

BASQUE DISHES

The Basque coast gives rise to superb seafood dishes, such as *bacalao al pil-pil* (cod and garlic in an olive-oil emulsion; pictured below) and *chipirones en su tinta* (baby squid in its own ink), while the hills are the source of *chuleton* (steaks) and Idiazabal cheese.

Pintxos

Enter any bar in the region, and the counter is sure to be groaning under the weight of a small mountain of tiny plates of culinary art. These are *pintxos* (Basque tapas), which will redefine your interpretation of the bar snack. The best are often the hot ones made to order.

HOW TO... Pay the Bill

You won't be brought the bill until you ask for it. Catch your server's attention and say, '*La cuenta, por favor*'.

Splitting the bill: Before taking payment, your server may ask you '*¿juntos o por separado*' (together or separately?). Splitting the bill is not always permitted.

Tipping: In restaurants, most locals tip up to 5%. A tip of around 10% is considered generous. It's not always possible to add a tip to a credit-card payment, so leave cash instead. It isn't necessary to tip in bars or cafes, though tips are always welcome.

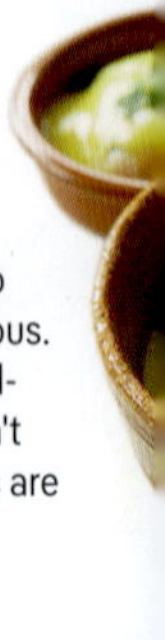

PRICE RANGES

The following price ranges refer to the cost of an average main course.

€ less than €12

€€ €12–20

€€€ more than €20

OPENING HOURS

Coffee shops 9am to 3pm Monday to Saturday

Restaurants 1pm to 4pm and 7pm to 11pm; some close Sunday night and/or Monday

***Pinxto* bars** 11am to midnight; most close at 4pm Sunday

Going Out

While the Basque Country might not be famous for its nightlife, a lot is happening if you know where to look.

Cafes Old-school neighbourhood cafes can be charming places, but the coffee is often mediocre. If you are fussy about your beans, look for a coffee shop. Many now use locally roasted beans and offer a range of brewing techniques.

Bars Some locals start early, and having a midday beer or glass of *txakoli* wine won't attract sideways looks. But the bar scene really gets going in the evening, from around 8pm, when people spill out onto the streets, drink in hand. At traditional bars, most people drink beer or wine but look too for *vermuterías* (vermouth bars) and cocktail bars.

Nightclubs If you're keen to hit the clubs, wait until at least 1am. Some clubs charge an entry fee. The drinking and dancing go on until around 6am.

HOW MUCH FOR A

Glass of *txakoli* wine €2.50

Gilda (olive and anchovy *pintxo*) €2

Palmera pastry €3

Pintxo of tortilla €3

Scoop of ice cream €3

Cup of coffee €2

Beer €2.50

LGBTIQ+ Travellers

Though the Basque Country is not particularly known for its LGBTIQ+ scene, travellers can expect to feel safe and welcome as they explore.

LGBTIQ+ Scene

Donostia-San Sebastián has long been an LGBTIQ-friendly destination, but these days, few places cater specifically to the community. The approach seems to be that since the city embraces diversity, is open to the community and is a safe place for LGBTIQ+ people to be, there is no particular need for separate spaces or club nights. One exception is **Dioni's** (p114), which hosts an LGBTIQ+ disco on Friday and Saturday nights.

Bilbao is also a generally LGBTIQ-friendly city. Casco Viejo has several LGBTIQ+ bars. On Friday nights, catch cabaret performances by drag queens.

Las Fellini at Badulake in Bilbao la Vieja. The city's biggest LGBTIQ+ party is at **El Balcón de la Lola** (p46) on Friday and Saturday nights.

OUR PICKS

Pride

The region's biggest Pride celebration is **Bilbao Bizkaia HARRO** (bilbaobizkaiapride.com) in June, involving a week of concerts, parades and events in Bilbao and Getxo. Beyond organising the Pride events, Bilbao Bizkaia HARRO works year-round to support the community and promote LGBTIQ+ rights. The website lists upcoming LGBTIQ+ parties.

CULTURAL CENTRE

In Donostia-San Sebastián, the **Tabakalera** (p135) cultural centre often hosts exhibitions, talks and film screenings of particular interest to the LGBTIQ+ community. Check the website to see what's on.

FEMINIST EVENTS SPACE

Check out the upcoming events at feminist cafe **La Sinsorga** (p46). The schedule features music, workshops and talks covering LGBTIQ+ themes.

Resources

- **revistablue.com** Monthly Spanish-language magazine for the Basque Country's LGBT community.
- **pikaramagazine.com** Spanish- and Basque-language feminist magazine with thought-provoking pieces on issues affecting the LGBTIQ+ community.
- **felgtbi.org** LGBTIQ+ advocacy group based in Madrid but has affiliated groups in Bilbao and Donostia-San Sebastián.

Health & Safe Travel

Bilbao and Donostia-San Sebastián are generally safe to visit, but it's always best to stay aware of your surroundings.

DRIVING

Police can issue on-the-spot fines for driving offences, including speeding. If you pay the fine within 20 days, it is reduced by 50%. The legal blood alcohol limit for driving in Spain is 0.5g of alcohol per litre of blood. Police carry out roadside checks for alcohol and drugs.

Beach Safety

The Basque Country is popular with surfers for a reason, but its large waves and undertows can be dangerous. Always swim in the designated areas and obey lifeguards' instructions. Green flags mean the waters are calm and it's safe to swim. Yellow flags indicate the possibility of strong currents or high waves. You can't swim, but you can put your feet in. Red flags mean swimming is prohibited because of dangerous conditions.

Tap Water

Tap water is safe to drink in Bilbao, San Sebastián and neighbouring areas.

Hill Walking

The weather in the Basque Country can change quickly. If you are going hiking, wear suitable footwear and bring extra layers of clothing, water and snacks. Protect yourself from the sun with a hat and sunscreen. Have a map so you can find your way if clouds roll in.

POLICE REPORT

If you are the victim of a minor crime in which you aren't threatened and there are no witnesses, you can request a police report online (denuncias.policia.es/OVD).

QUICK INFO

Cannabis
Cannabis has been decriminalised but only for personal use and in small quantities.

Security
Don't leave anything of value in your car, especially near the beach.

Cycling
You can be fined for using a mobile phone while cycling.

Responsible Travel

Follow these tips to leave a lighter footprint, support local and have a positive impact on communities.

Recycling

Waste is separated for recycling throughout the Basque Country. Recycling bins are colour coded: brown for organic (food) waste, yellow for plastic and cans, blue for paper and cardboard, and green with round holes for glass. White bins are for textiles. Non-recyclable waste goes in the grey bins in Donostia-San Sebastián. In Bilbao, the non-recyclable waste bins are black with green lids.

Water Fountains

Find water fountains all over Bilbao, Donostia-San Sebastián, and the towns and villages of the Basque coast. Bring a reusable bottle to refill on the go.

FROM LEFT: FOTOADICTA/SHUTTERSTOCK ©, DONALD THOREBY/SHUTTERSTOCK ©

OUR PICK

Birdlife

Learn about migratory birds and the importance of the Urdaibai Biosphere Reserve ecosystem at the **Urdaibai Bird Center** (p92), which aims to protect the birds and their habitats.

Sustainable Fashion

For preowned clothes in retro styles, browse the shelves of **La Soupe by Vintage Closet** (p115) in Donostia-San Sebastián and **Supernova Vintage** (p47) in Bilbao's Casco Viejo. The garments at Bilbao store **Ätakontu** (p47) are designed and manufactured locally using organic cotton. Nearby, **Libertad Avenue** (p47) specialises in handmade sustainable footwear for urban cyclists.

Resources

• **slowfoodbilbaobizkaia.es** Lists local restaurants that meet the sustainability criteria to be considered Km0. • **ihobe.eus** The Basque government's environmental management company.

AZURMENDI

Near Bilbao, chef Eneko Atxa's three-Michelin-starred restaurant **Azurmendi** (azurmendi.restaurant) has won acclaim for its sustainable practices as well as its outstanding food. The bioclimatic restaurant building features a rooftop vegetable garden and rainwater tanks.

Local & Seasonal

One of the joys of the Basque Country is its bounty of fresh, locally sourced produce. You can buy directly from growers at Bilbao's Saturday morning **Gure Lurreko Merkatua** farmers market in **Arenal** (p42). Bilbao's **Mercado de la Ribera** (p40) has fresh produce stalls, including one specialising in local mushrooms. In San Sebastián, see what's on offer at **Mercado de la Bretxa** (p107) and **Mercado San Martín** (p131). Shop for local cheeses, wines and tinned fish at **Conservas Hondarribia** (p155). In Zarautz, look for local produce at **Merkatu Plaza** (p95).

SECONDHAND MARKET

Donostiatruk is a secondhand market at **Tabakalera** (p135) in Donostia-San Sebastián. It takes place on the third Saturday of every month from 10am to 2pm.

Climate Change & Travel

It's impossible to ignore the impact we have when travelling; Lonely Planet urges all travellers to engage with their travel carbon footprint, which will mainly come from air travel. While there often isn't an alternative, travellers can look to minimise the number of flights they take, opt for newer aircrafts and use cleaner ground transport, such as trains. One proposed solution—purchasing carbon offsets—unfortunately does not cancel out the impact of individual flights. While most destinations will depend on air travel for the foreseeable future, for now, pursuing ground-based travel where possible is the best course of action.

The **UN Carbon Offset Calculator** shows how flying impacts a household's emissions

The **ICAO's carbon emissions calculator** allows visitors to analyse the CO_2 generated by point-to-point journeys

Accessible Travel

Public Transport

Bilbao's metro was designed to be accessible, with station lifts, wide gates, and space onboard for wheelchairs and prams. All Bilbobus buses in Bilbao and Dbuses in Donostia-San Sebastián are wheelchair accessible. On Dbus services, upcoming stops are announced over a speaker and shown on a screen.

Adaptive Surf Lessons

Based in Donostia-San Sebastián, the agency **Bask For All** (baskforall.com) offers a range of accessible tours in the Basque Country, as well as activities such as adaptive surf lessons tailored to meet the needs of people with disabilities.

WHEELCHAIRS & SCOOTERS

In Bilbao, you can rent wheelchairs, mobility scooters and other mobility equipment from **Abuelo Actual** (abueloactual.com). On its website, click *alquileres* for available options. Contact the company to arrange delivery.

Sign-Dance

Look out for events in Bilbao and San Sebastián staged by **Arymux** (arymux.com), an inclusive and accessible theatre and dance company that fuses sign language with performances of theatre, dance, music and poetry.

OUR PICK

At **Playa de la Concha** (p120), a free **assisted bathing** service uses amphibious vehicles to transport people with mobility issues over the sand and into the sea. Find it near the lifeguard station by the clocks.

A further **barrier-free bathing** service for people with disabilities is provided by **Fundación Hegalak-Zabalik** (+34 943 433 680; hegalak.com), whose staff have specialist training and access to buggies and cranes. It's free, but you need to make an appointment.

ACCESSIBLE THEATRE

In Bilbao, **Sala BBK** (salabbk.bbk.eus) has installed an electromagnetic induction loop system, allowing people with hearing difficulties to better pick up the sound with their hearing aids.

Resources

- **accesible.visitbiscay.eus** Accessibility information for Bilbao and Biscay in English.
- **accessibility.sansebastianturismoa.eus** Accessibility guide compiled by Donostia-San Sebastián's tourism office in English.

Nuts & Bolts

Opening Hours

Banks 9am to 2pm Monday to Friday

Nightclubs Midnight or 1am to 5am or 6am

Post offices 8.30am to 2.30pm and 4.30pm to 8pm Monday to Friday; larger branches open through lunch

Restaurants Lunch 1pm to 4pm; dinner 8.30pm to 11pm or midnight

Shops 10am to 2pm and 4.30pm to 7.30pm or 5pm to 8pm Monday to Saturday; supermarkets and department stores 9am or 10am to 9pm Monday to Saturday. Some supermarkets open 10am to 9pm Sunday.

Abierto / irekita
Open

Cerrado / itxita
Closed

QUICK INFO

Time zone Central European time (GMT/UTC plus one hour)

Calling code 94 (Bilbao); 943 (Donostia-San Sebastián)

Emergency number 112

Population 342,000 (Bilbao); 183,000 (San Sebastián)

ELECTRICITY

230V/50Hz

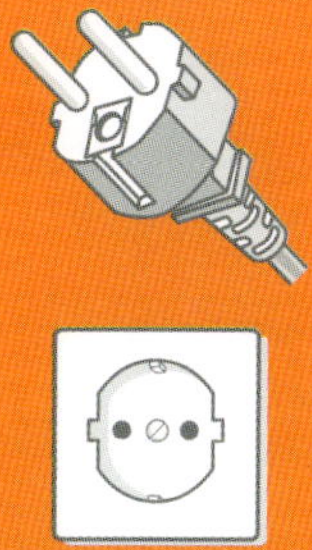

Smoking

Smoking is banned in all enclosed public spaces. It is common for people to smoke outside bars and restaurants. Smoking is also banned on some beaches, including those in Lekeitio, Mundaka, Zarautz, Getaria, Hondarribia and Zumaia. Smoke-free beaches have signs with warnings of potential fines.

Public Holidays

Año Nuevo (New Year's Day) 1 January

Día de los Reyes Magos (Epiphany) 6 January

Jueves Santo (Maundy Thursday) March/April

Viernes Santo (Good Friday) March/April

Lunes de Pascua (Easter Monday) March/April

Fiesta del Trabajador (Labour Day) 1 May

Día de Santiago Apóstol (Feast of St James the Apostle) 25 July

La Asunción (Feast of the Assumption) 15 August

Fiesta Nacional (National Day) 12 October

Día de Todos los Santos (All Saints Day) 1 November

Día de la Constitución (Constitution Day) 6 December

La Inmaculada Concepción (Feast of the Immaculate Conception) 8 December

Navidad (Christmas) 25 December

Language

Basics

Hello.
Hola. *o·la*

Goodbye.
Adiós. *a·dyos*

How are you?
¿Qué tal? *ke tal*

Fine, thanks.
Bien, gracias. *byen gra·thyas*

Please.
Por favor. *por fa·vor*

Thank you.
Gracias. *gra·thyas*

Excuse me.
Perdón. *per·don*

Sorry.
Lo siento. *lo syen·to*

Yes./No.
Sí./No. *see/no*

Eating & Drinking

I'm a vegetarian. (m/f)
Soy vegetariano/a *soy ve·khe·ta·rya·no/a*

Cheers!
¡Salud! *sa·loo*

That was delicious!
¡Estaba buenísimo! *es·ta·ba bwe·nee·see·mo*

Please bring the bill.
Por favor nos trae la cuenta. *por fa·vor nos tra·e la kwen·ta*

I'd like ...	**Quisiera ...** *kee·sye·ra ...*
a coffee	**un café** *oon ka·fe*
a table	**una mesa** *oo·na me·sa*
for two	**para dos** *pa·ra dos*
a wine	**un vino** *oon vee·no*
two beers	**dos cervezas** *dos ther·ve·thas*

EMERGENCIES

Help! **¡Socorro!** so·ko·ro

Call a doctor! **¡Llame a un médico!** lya·me a oon me·dee·ko

Call the police! **¡Llame a la policía!** lya·me a la po·lee·thee·a

I'm lost. (m/f) **Estoy perdido/a.** es·toy per·dee·do/a

I'm ill. (m/f) **Estoy enfermo/a.** es·toy en·fer·mo/a

Where are the toilets?
¿Dónde están los baños?
don·de es·tan los ba·nyos.

Numbers

1 **uno** *oo·no*

2 **dos** *dos*

3 **tres** *tres*

4 **cuatro** *kwa·tro*

5 **cinco** *theen·ko*

Spanish vs Basque

Spanish *(español)* – often referred to as *castellano* (Castilian) to distinguish it from other languages spoken in Spain – is the most widely understood language across the country. Basque *(euskara)* is spoken in the Basque Country *(el país vasco)* and is one of the four official languages of Spain. Speaking Spanish in Basque-speaking cities such as Bilbao and Donostia-San Sebastián will generally be expected from a foreigner. Travellers who learn a little Spanish should be relatively well understood.

Most Spanish sounds are pronounced the same as their English counterparts. Just read our pronunciation guides as if they were English and you'll be understood. Note that 'm/f' indicates masculine and feminine forms.

TIME

What time is it?
¿Qué hora es?
ke o·ra es

It's (10) o'clock.
Son (las diez).
son (las dyeth)

morning **mañana**
ma·nya·na

afternoon **tarde**
tar·de

evening **noche**
no·che

yesterday **ayer** *a·yer*

today **hoy** *oy*

tomorrow **mañana**
ma·nya·na

Shopping

I'd like to buy ...
Quisiera comprar ...
kee·sye·ra kom·prar ...

May I look at it?
¿Puedo verlo?
pwe·do ver·lo

How much is it?
¿Cuánto cuesta?
kwan·to kwes·ta

That's too/very expensive.
Es muy caro.
es mooy ka·ro

Transport & Directions

Where's ...?
¿Dónde está ...?
don·de es·ta ...

What's the address?
¿Cuál es la dirección? *kwal es la dee·rek·thyon*

Can you show me (on the map)?
¿Me lo puede indicar (en el mapa)? *me lo pwe·de een·dee·kar (en el ma·pa)*

I want to go to ... **Quisiera ir a ...** *kee·sye·ra eer a ...*

What time does it arrive/leave?
¿A qué hora llega/sale? *a ke o·ra lye·ga/sa·le*

I want to get off here. **Quiero bajarme aquí.** *kye·ro ba·khar·me a·kee*

6	7	8	9	10
seis *seys*	**siete** *sye·te*	**ocho** *o·cho*	**nueve** *nwe·ve*	**diez** *dyeth*

Index

Sights p000 Map pages ***p000***

See also separate subindexes for:
Eating p173
Drinking p174
Shopping p175

Eating

Drinking

Shopping

Send Us Your Feedback

We love to hear from travellers – your comments help make our books better. We read every word, and we guarantee that your feedback goes straight to the authors. Visit lonelyplanet.com/contact to submit your updates and suggestions.

Note: We may edit, reproduce and incorporate your comments in Lonely Planet products such as guidebooks, websites and digital products, so let us know if you are happy to have your name acknowledged. For a copy of our privacy policy visit lonelyplanet.com/legal.

Acknowledgements

Cover photograph: Donostia-San Sebastián. Sergii Figurnyi/ Shutterstock ©

Back photograph: *pintxos*. Francesco Bonino/ Shutterstock ©

THIS BOOK

Destination Editor
Annemarie McCarthy

Cartographer
Rachel Imeson

Production Editor
Megan Graieg

Book Designer
Compton Sheldon

Assisting Editors
Lauren Keith, Fionnuala Twomey

Cover Researcher
Marc Backwell

Thanks to
Ronan Abayawickrema, Alison Killilea, Kate Mathews, Jenna Myers

Published by Lonely Planet Global Limited

CRN 554153

5th edition – Feb 2025

ISBN 9781837583317

10 9 8 7 6 5 4 3 2 1

Printed in China